Info-Flood

Info-Flood

How to Swim in a Sea of
Information Without Going Under

Marlene Caroselli, Ed. D.

SkillPath Publications

Mission, KS

Project Editor: Kelly Scanlon

Copyeditor: Jennifer Dick

Page Layout: Premila Malik Borchardt and Rod Hankins

Cover Design: Rod Hankins

Library of Congress Catalog Card Number: 96-070931

ISBN: 1-57294-041-7

10   9   8   7   6   5   4   3   2   1   97   98   99   00   01

Printed in the United States of America

Contents

v

Introduction

"We are drowning in information but starved for knowledge!" Author John Naisbitt's words reflect a common cry. Daily, a stream of information is directed at us—so much so that we sometimes feel we are drowning in it. Indeed, it is hard to keep our heads above this data-drenched "water." The feeling of being in too deep, the fear of sinking, the difficulty of catching one's breath—all of these metaphoric conditions are common in today's world.

Can the information be translated into knowledge? Not all of it, and this mismatch between what we receive and what we can use prompts observations such as Naisbitt's. The problem is perhaps best illustrated by the story of a middle manager in a large corporation, a man who received voluminous amounts of computer-generated data. He was expected to review data and then pass it along to the next person on the routing list. The manager had a gnawing suspicion that others on the list probably did what he did: cursorily skim the material and pass it along.

One day he decided to confirm his suspicions by placing a note in the middle of the stack before sending it along.

The note read:

"If anyone reads this far, call me at extension 49. I will give you $100." *He did not receive a single call.*

Causes of Info-Flood

Is it any wonder we feel inundated? We are being swept away with data, drowned in a sea of facts. Between print media and electronic media, we experience tremendous information pressure. In fact, futurists predict that within the next twenty-five years, information pressure will be thirty-two times greater than it is today. (The number of cable channels alone, for example, will soon reach five hundred!)

The explosion of information and the access to it are mildly depressing realities for knowledge workers—and we are a nation of knowledge workers. To illustrate, a noted consultant in the field of Total Quality Management once remarked that she would probably die before she could read every book on the topic. That's because more than 2,000 titles abound. And that figure will continue to grow, as will titles in related fields, such as team building, benchmarking, and ISO-9000.

Effects of Info-Flood

One of the effects of having too much information is our tendency to disregard it. As a result, those with messages to deliver must fight their way into the mind of an audience. For example, imagine you an advertiser who paid a substantial sum to promote your product during commercials aired during a popular television miniseries.

A recent poll asked 100 viewers about such commercials. Here is what people remembered about them:

- 32 percent of the viewers remembered the ad for Kodak film.

- 32 percent remembered the ad for Prudential.

- 26 percent remembered seeing a Mobil Oil ad.

- 23 percent remembered an ad for Budweiser beer.

- 19 percent remembered an ad for Volkswagen cars.

- 18 percent remembered seeing an ad for American Express.

And yet not one of those companies advertised during the miniseries.

Stress is another effect of the tremendous amount of information we are exposed to each day. We feel fragmented, torn in many directions, and overcommitted. We feel, quite simply, that we don't have enough time to receive, digest, and use the information we have at our fingertips. As an example, by the year 2000, experts tell us there will be more than 1 million professional journals available. Treading the knowledge-waters in one's chosen field could be a full-time job itself.

Finally, we find paradoxes created by the information-influx. We are being asked to do more with less (and computers certainly help us to do this). And yet, we are asked to learn more and more about less and less. As a nation, we have created specializations within specializations so that even though our ability to communicate across long distances has grown remarkably, our ability to communicate with each other has diminished considerably. In addition, in the midst of this knowledge explosion, more and more professionals are finding that useful knowledge related to their work is truly a *perishable* commodity. Consider engineers, for example. Within five years, half the job-related knowledge they possess will be obsolete. Throughout this book, other information-related paradoxes business people face will be explored.

Vocabulary Related to Info-Flood

Info-Flood is not a technocrat's guide. This book will not make you technically literate. It is not filled with techno-babble. Its purpose is to help you cope with the flood of information that washes over each of us—information from *numerous* sources, not just computer sources, electronic transmissions, or cyberspace communications. Become as familiar as you can with techno-terms, however, because the technology and the language that is the coin of its realm are here to stay. These terms include the following:

Bulletin boards. Electronic means of posting information for general consumption.

Commercial on-line services. Companies such as America Online, Prodigy, CompuServe, and Genie that organize information electronically for users.

Distance learning. Electronic education by way of teleconferencing and computer on-line classes.

E-mail. Service that permits private and individual communications, giving both the sender's and the receiver's electronic address.

Hypertext (also called "hot text" or "interactive text"). A means of cross-referencing information through electronic linking.

Internet. The mother of all computer networks.

Newsgroups. Electronic gatherings of people with common interests and expertise.

Virtual reality. The ability to interact with other locations without actually being in them.

World Wide Web. Part of the Internet that is organized by home pages (electronic storefronts).

To avoid falling into an alphabetic abyss, learn some of the more familiar acronyms:

ATM	Asynchronous Transfer Mode
EDI	Electronic Data Interchange
EDMS	Electronic Document Management System
FAQ	Frequently Asked Questions
FTP	File Transfer Protocol
HTML	Hypertext Markup Language
ISDN	Integrated Services Digital Network
LAN	Local Area Network
URL	Uniform Resource Locator
WAN	Wide Area Network

Here are some terms that appear repeatedly in *Info-Flood:*

Info-addicts (or knowledge-junkies). Refers to people who are data-collectors, people who are obsessed with possessing knowledge on a great many topics. In essence, they suffer from *info-addictions.*

Info-angst (or info-stress). Refers to the anxious feeling produced by facing a great deal of information and the task of converting that information to another form or location.

Info-flood (or info-bog, info-swamp, info-glut). Refers to the deluge of information from numerous sources that washes over us each day.

Information and knowledge. These terms are used interchangeably throughout the book, with full acknowledgment of the distinction to which Naisbitt alludes. *Information* is generally regarded as an accumulation of data without any connections among the data or any new insights derived from analysis of the data. *Knowledge* is generally regarded as new insights or profound advances in the established thinking of a particular field.

Organization of the Book

The book is organized into seven chapters, each titled with a strong verb.

Define (Chapter 1) encourages you to diagnose coping strategies on three levels: individual, team, and organization. Without diagnosis, there can be no prescription.

Align (Chapter 2) assists you in establishing what's important in your life, and also what's important to others who affect your life—such as managers and strategic planners within your organization. Additionally, you are asked to think about *inclinations*—what you're inclined to do, what the organization is inclined to do, what the industry you work in is likely to pursue—and then think about ways to align these trends with your own direction.

Streamline (Chapter 3) asks you to think about the "vital few" and the "trivial many" tasks that constitute your day. Techniques for establishing priorities are presented here as well as tips for optimizing your time.

Refine (Chapter 4) asks you to take a new look at the priorities you've established and to define them further via milestones, conferences, and reassessments.

Confine (Chapter 5) directs you to think about skills you will need in the future and to tolerate the inevitable paradoxes that constitute life in the Information Age. This chapter also provides tips for becoming more organized.

Decline (Chapter 6) refers to an action you can perform firmly but gracefully, whether you are dealing with people, your preferences, or your own drive toward perfectionism. Learning to be selective is the crux of this chapter.

Outline (Chapter 7) helps you beat a path through excessive verbiage by using visual maps, outlining methods, and a formula for advancing the action. It also encourages you to resist info-acquisition urges, to exert control over those forces that seek to imprison you in the paper penitentiary.

The Conclusion reviews the essential thrust of each chapter and offers you a final opportunity to take "swimming lessons."

Interviews at the end of each of these chapters offer valuable coping strategies used by individuals who are successfully keeping their heads above water in the ever-rising Sea of Information.

Finally, paralleling the "factoids" that Cable News Network uses to capture viewer interest, you will find factoids (statistics about Info-Flood), queryoids (questions for you to consider), quotoids (quotations about the knowledge explosion), and predictoids (predictions about Info-Flood) scattered throughout the margins of the book. These are included to emphasize the depth of the flood and to motivate you to remain afloat in spite of it.

The book uses the water metaphor (and occasionally the vehicular metaphor prompted by the Information Superhighway). The references to these graphic images are deliberate. Scientists have found that visual information is not only easier to remember than verbal information but also increases over time. (In other words, if you are given twelve visual images today and twelve words, you might only remember six images and six words a week from now. But two weeks from now, you could remember eight images yet only three words.) The term for this remarkable recall is *hypermnesia*.

The subtext of this book is a message of hope. As overwhelming as it sometimes seems to keep afloat in this ocean of data, it is possible to remain calm among the turbulence. There is no denying the importance of being informed in the Information Age that we live in. And because technology tends to beget more technology, we need to assume responsibility for learning how to use the cellular network, learning what groupware can do for you, learning about cellular digital packet data, and things of this ilk. The longer you wait to learn about them, the further behind you'll get.

This book is a prescription for those in danger of drowning. It is designed as a life jacket to keep you afloat. Take full advantage of the "power swimming lessons" offered here—your old strokes simply won't suffice any longer.

If you feel data-drenched on a regular basis, if you have trouble separating the data from the dross, if you tried "management by surfing around" but felt like a canoe paddler on a transoceanic trip, then you're doing the right thing by reading *Info-Flood*. In these pages, you'll find dozens of ideas for transforming your canoe into a powerboat.

Reading this book is like drinking water: swallowing too much at once won't help digestion. In other words, don't try to read the book in one sitting. Instead, read a chapter and give yourself time to try out the techniques before trying to swallow more.

Define

1

When you consider the facts surrounding the knowledge explosion, like most people, you are bound to feel you need help. Consider these statistics, for example:

- Fifty percent of all projects employees have undertaken are actually behind schedule.

- Each week, 145 pages of information cross the desk of the average employee.

- In 1991, organizations expended more money on computing and communications equipment than the combined money expended for industrial, farm, construction, and mining equipment.

Factoid

We now have nearly 150 million e-mail addresses, cellular phones, pagers, fax machines, voice mailboxes, and answering machines—up 365 percent from 40.7 million in 1987.

Before you can decide how much help or what kind of help you need in order to survive the current information deluge, it's important to define what the problem actually is. Then, you can set a course of action based on needs that have been assessed rather than assumptions that haven't been verified. This chapter helps you make diagnoses on three levels: individual, team, and organization.

Individual

Begin by taking the following quiz to find out how you currently handle information and where you're headed. Will you be enlightened or burned by the explosion of knowledge occurring all around you?

Quiz:
• •
Self-Diagnosis

Respond "yes" or "no" to the following items.

Yes   **No**

☐   ☐   1. At the end of many days, I feel I've frittered away my time.

☐   ☐   2. I often feel I will never be caught up.

☐   ☐   3. More and more, things seem to "fall through the cracks."

☐   ☐   4. I find it increasingly more difficult to locate things.

☐   ☐   5. I have mistakenly overlooked or not paid attention to important information.

☐   ☐   6. I often go to meetings not fully prepared and leave meetings feeling I have neither made an important contribution nor learned valuable information.

☐   ☐   7. It depresses me to think I will never be able to learn everything there is to know about a field that interests me (such as computers).

☐   ☐   8. I worry that my children (or young people in general) aren't being taught how to find their way in these new intellectual frontiers.

Factoid

By the turn of the century, American firms will file 120 billion new sheets of paper a year.

▼

☐ ☐ 9. I have some files I haven't looked at in at least three months.

☐ ☐ 10. The information in some of my files is probably outdated.

How Well Did You Do?

Score of 0-3 "Yes" answers: The knowledge explosion presents no danger to you at all. You're being warmed by its heat, attracted by its spectacle, but you aren't being burned by its intensity.

Score of 4-6 "Yes" answers: You need to increase your coping skills. Reading this book and applying the techniques provided should help you take advantage of the many benefits the knowledge explosion offers.

Score of 7-10 "Yes" answers: Your existing skills need to be updated, and you need to add new skills for dealing with the power generated by the knowledge explosion.

If you scored in the 0-3 category, you are a rare person indeed. If you answered "yes," though, to four or more items, consider one of the following improvement tips designed to help you manage your time and information:

Keep a time log. You may *think* you know how the time of your life is being spent, but you will be surprised to discover what the time log reveals. The logging form need not be elaborate nor difficult to use, but it should be maintained for a period of several weeks.

Organize your files. Several weeks a year are lost by people searching for lost or misfiled records. Add time to your work life by tossing those files you no longer use and by organizing those you do. Invest the time now—it will yield big temporal profits in the future.

Clean off your desk. For most people, the sight of a cluttered desk adds to the feeling of being fragmented. And, when all those little piles are staring at us, we are tempted to poke a finger (or poke a nose) into them. Thus, we sometimes scatter our mental energy and our time, instead of concentrating on an important task.

Ask not to attend meetings that have little value for you. It will require some gumption on your part, but this *is* the era of empowerment. If you are deriving little and contributing little, explain how your time might be maximized if it could be spent on something else. Or, have ready some creative alternatives, such as sending an "alter ego" to select meetings.

Speak with knowledgeable colleagues about the future skills that will be most important in your field. Even with as much reading as you may do, you simply cannot read everything being written about skills that will be most valuable in the years ahead. Find time to discuss future needs with someone from the human resources department or perhaps even with your own manager in order to stay abreast of trends and the predictions of futurists.

Predictoid

The number of cable channels will soon reach 500.

Improvement Exercise:
Self

Choose one of the tips below that you feel you can implement right away. Then answer the questions regarding a plan of action.

☐ Keep a time log.

☐ Organize your files.

☐ Clean off your desk.

☐ Ask not to attend meetings that have little value for you.

☐ Speak with knowledgeable colleagues about the future skills that will be most important in your field.

1. Briefly explain what you will do:

_____

_____

_____

_____

_____

_____

_____

2. What barriers will you need to overcome?

_____

_____

_____

_____

Quotoid

Isaac Asimov: "I am not a speed reader. I am a speed understander."

◄

3. Who will assist you?

_____

_____

_____

_____

4. When will you start?

_____

_____

_____

_____

5. How will you reward yourself for lessening your Info-Angst?

_____

_____

_____

_____

Team

Info-Flood can impact a team's productivity as profoundly as it can impact an individual's. Teams that haven't deliberated about what data need to be collected may subsequently waste time on data that need *not* be collected. Another nonproductive scenario involves teams that collect too much data. They suffer "paralysis by analysis." Other teams are deterred from moving forward because of the sheer weight of the data available.

Take the following quiz to learn whether your team is using information both wisely and well.

Quiz:
Team Diagnosis

Respond "yes" or "no" to the following items:

Yes   **No**

☐   ☐   1. Our team meetings always include an agenda.

☐   ☐   2. The agenda is sent out in advance so people can come to meetings prepared.

☐   ☐   3. We have prepared a set of ground rules for our meetings.

☐   ☐   4. Those ground rules are posted in our meeting room.

☐   ☐   5. Team assignments are made during the meeting.

☐   ☐   6. Minutes (that include those assignments) are sent out soon after the meeting has taken place.

☐   ☐   7. When we need data, we check first to see if it's already been compiled by others.

☐   ☐   8. The team leader or facilitator ensures that discussion isn't dominated by any one person and that it's related to the topic at hand.

Factoid

Seventy-five percent of workers will need more training to keep up with the changing requirements of their jobs.

▼

☐   ☐   9. We have on our team (or invite to our meetings) someone with a basic knowledge of statistics.

☐   ☐   10. We limit our data collection to vital issues.

How Well Did Your Team Do?

Score of 0-3 "Yes" answers: Training is a must for your team. You are probably wasting time, energy, and organizational resources. You can easily find hope and help, however, and turn your floundering efforts around.

Score of 4-6 "Yes" answers: You have probably realized some mild successes, but you haven't yet tapped the full potential of team members. Do one or more of the improvement exercises that follow (see pp. 24-25) and note any changes in the way your team operates.

Score of 7-10 "Yes" answers: Your team functions as an integrated unit, respectful of the uses of data but not overly dependent on them.

If you scored in the 7-10 category, you are no doubt part of an experienced, high-performing team. In fact, you may be ready to expand your capabilities by way of groupware. Take a look at some characteristics of this latest type of software and see if your firm may be interested.

Factoid

There were fewer than one million fax machines in use in America in 1988. Today there are more than 14 million.

- Hundreds of products on the market today offer groups the opportunity to work together electronically, no matter where they are located. So a team member who is traveling or at home could still "attend" team meetings.

- Groupware differs from e-mail in that it allows you to forward information to the proper bulletin board. Anyone who needs information about a subject checks that bulletin board to find it.

- A study in 1991 by a major aircraft company found that groupware could reduce by 90 percent the time it took to complete a project. While the cost for such tools may be high, so is the cost of meeting for ten months to complete a project when the project could be done in one month using the software.

- Electronic access to information and to interpersonal communications can dramatically affect how teams operate. A *Fortune* article ("Groupware Goes Boom," December 27, 1993, p. 100) describes how an accounting firm put together a proposal for a multimillion-dollar consulting contract in just four days. By doing so, they beat a competitor who had been preparing a bid for weeks. The article also describes how an advertising agency used the software to track the extent of team members' contributions in order to compensate fairly. In this company, 15 percent to 20 percent of profits are paid to employees.

If you answered "yes" to three or fewer items on page 19, consider using one of the following improvement tips.

Invite a manager whom everyone respects to observe your team during one of its meetings. Chances are, the manager has had a great deal of experience working with and serving on teams. Even if this is not the case, however, the team can still profit from this outsider's observations, especially if defensiveness can be reduced enough for members to really listen.

Attend a class on team building. You will be able to pick up at least a dozen tips in such a class. If you put them to use immediately, you will be able to see immediate results. Don't rest on the success of your initial efforts, though. Seek to "continuously improve" the meeting process.

Read a book on how to improve the efficiency of teams. (See the Bibliography and Suggested Reading on page 171.) Although being in a class permits "hands-on" experience, the more passive act of reading can still yield valuable ideas. Find 52 recommendations and try one a week.

Prepare an evaluation form and use it at the end of every team meeting. The form could be based on the complaints you usually hear about the meeting process in your organization. So, for example, if people complain the meetings don't start on time, the first questions would relate to the starting time. The forms should have questions answerable by "yes" or "no" or other easy-to-use structures.

Find someone in the organization with data collection or data-reporting skills and ask that person to serve as a coach for your team. Somewhere in your organization is a person who has studied statistics and/or who has data-collection and data-reporting skills. Tap the expertise of this individual and be certain to show appreciation for his or her input.

Microchips double their performance capability every year and a half.

Improvement Exercise:
Team

Select an improvement tip you feel you can implement right away. Then answer the questions regarding a plan of action.

☐ Invite a manager whom everyone respects to observe your team during one of its meetings.

☐ Attend a class on team building.

☐ Read a book on how to improve the efficiency of teams.

☐ Prepare an evaluation form and use it at the end of every team meeting.

☐ Find someone in the organization with data collection or data-reporting skills and ask that person to serve as a coach for your team.

1. Briefly explain what you will do:

_____

_____

_____

_____

_____

_____

2. What barriers will you need to overcome?

_____

_____

_____

_____

3. Who will assist you?

_____

_____

_____

_____

4. When will you start?

_____

_____

_____

_____

_____

5. How will you reward yourself for lessening your Info-Angst?

_____

_____

_____

_____

_____

Queryoid

Are you an info-sponge, constantly absorbing data about the present, past, and the future?

▼

Organization

Has your organization entered the Information Age? If so, is it driven by data or drowning in data? Think honestly about yourself and the knowledge you have about your organization. Do you actively seek such knowledge? For example, do you ask to be informed about the financial realities that determine your organization's success or failure in the marketplace? If you possess such knowledge, do you share it with employees you supervise or manage? with colleagues? with team members?

Consider how far an organization can reach towards its goals when information is managed properly and shared at all levels of the organization:

- Jack Stack, the chief proponent of open-book management, turned his company, Springfield Remanufacturing Corp., from a $6 million company with 119 employees in 1983 to a $108 million company with more than 800 employees in 1995.

- Rick Hartsock, owner of Sandstrom Products, encourages people to creatively cooperate rather than simply complain. When a worker complained about wages, Hartsock asked if any other workers felt the same way. He was informed they did. Hartsock told the complaining employee to form a pay-plan committee and that he would approve any reasonable plan they devised. Employees at Sandstrom today continue to ask for things but are expected to submit cost justifications along with their requests (Source: "The Open-Book Revolution," by John Case, *Inc.*, June 1995, p. 40).

- For yet another unique way to use data effectively in an organization, consider this: The government systems branch of Sprint in Kansas City, Missouri, uses revenues per employee as one of several crucial financial criteria.

- The Herman Miller Co., a furniture manufacturer, explains financial terms and revenue realities to employees via videos to keep everyone informed.

Yet, despite these advantages of information sharing, a recent poll by Louis Harris found that fewer than one-third of employees polled felt the management of their organizations had established clear goals and directions. Is this because these organizations lack goals, or because they fail to share information with employees?

In a different study, the Forum Corp. found 82 percent of surveyed CEOs declared that their strategic plans were fully understood by "those who need to know." In your organization, to what extent are strategic plans fully understood? Who determines "those who need to know"? What determines "those who need to know"?

Take the quiz that follows to learn more about whether your organization is driven by data or drowning in it.

Quiz:
Organizational Diagnosis

Respond "yes" or "no" to the following items:

Yes   No

☐ ☐ 1. Managers in my organization typically make decisions based on data.

☐ ☐ 2. The rationale for those decisions is typically shared with employees throughout the organization.

☐ ☐ 3. A policy to reduce paperwork has been clearly articulated.

☐ ☐ 4. Employees generally feel empowered.

☐ ☐ 5. Team assignments are made during meetings.

☐ ☐ 6. Mission, vision, and values statements have been prepared by senior management.

☐ ☐ 7. Most employees are aware of these statements.

☐ ☐ 8. Employees realize the importance of aligning the work they do with the essence of these statements.

☐ ☐ 9. Most managers are aware of and practice "open book management."

☐ ☐ 10. Employees are periodically encouraged to take control of information; for example, by having a biannual "clean-out-your-files" day or by being asked not to misuse the e-mail system.

Factoid

More words are published weekly than were created from the beginning of history to 1800.

How Well Did Your Organization Do?

Score of 0-3 "Yes" answers: Your organization may be satisfying its customers, producing a quality product or service, and even increasing its annual revenues by amounts sufficient to please stakeholders. However, there is probably considerable room for improvement in the way information is handled internally.

Score of 4-6 "Yes" answers: It appears your organization is doing a fair job of disseminating important information and simultaneously supporting efforts to discard unimportant information. If so, then yours is probably the type of organization interested in continuous improvement. Take at least one of the Improvement Exercise suggestions on pages 31 to 32 to your manager or implement one yourself.

Score of 7-10 "Yes" answers: In terms of information management, yours is probably an outstanding company—cognizant of both the uses and the abuses to be derived from easy access to information. (You probably do not have to contend with "silo-ism"—the management style that keeps knowledge in and people out—and can proudly declare that managers in your organization do not practice it.)

If your score was three or fewer "yes" answers, select one of the following tips designed to improve the flow of information in your organization.

Read *The Great Game of Business* by Jack Stack. This best-seller details the importance of financial knowledge—for *every* employee. Write a "book report" and share it with colleagues—perhaps at the next staff meeting.

Obtain copies of the organizational mission, vision, and values statements. If they don't exist, ask your manager if you could form a team to develop them for your work unit or department. Think of ways to make others aware of what your company stands for.

Benchmark. Place calls to other companies (with your boss's approval) to learn how they handle the paradox of sharing more (relevant) information and working with less information.

Plan lunchtime lectures so employees can learn more about the financial conditions that drive the organization.

Educate yourself about financial terms and what they mean in your organization. Then translate your knowledge into a readily digestible format for co-workers.

Improvement Exercise:
Organization

- ☐ Read *The Great Game of Business* by Jack Stack.
- ☐ Obtain copies of the organizational mission, vision, and values statements.
- ☐ Benchmark.
- ☐ Plan lunchtime lectures so employees can learn more about the financial conditions that drive the organization.
- ☐ Educate yourself about financial terms and what they mean in your organization.

1. Briefly explain what you will do:

_____

_____

_____

_____

_____

_____

_____

_____

_____

Predictoid

Every human on the planet will be Internet-connected by 2001.

▼

2. What barriers will you need to overcome?

_____

_____

_____

_____

3. Who will assist you?

_____

_____

_____

_____

4. When will you start?

_____

_____

_____

_____

5. How can you gauge any improvements in the way your organization is disseminating and discarding information?

_____

_____

_____

_____

Summary

The diagnoses you have conducted have, ideally, sharpened your awareness of information needs—for you, your team, and your organization. You probably didn't achieve an excellent score in all three categories. For this reason, numerous suggestions were supplied— ideas that you can implement as you work to improve the way you and your larger work unit access, digest, and use the information that abounds in our society.

In general, management experts agree that the more employees understand about revenues, profits, and costs, the more empowered they feel. An empowered work force seeks enlightenment—whether or not profit-sharing or employee-ownership programs are in place. You can engage in a variety of actions to attain that enlightenment. Even in gestures as simple as reading the annual report and asking questions about entries you don't understand, you expand your general understanding as well as your feeling that you are truly part of the organization.

With so much information available, it's essential that you make choices and remain centered despite the forces that would throw you off balance. Remember to keep the big picture in mind as you make those choices.

Interview with Dorothy Pecoraro, Director, School-to-Work Transition Program, City School District, Rochester, New York

As one looks at the workplace of the twenty-first century, it's evident that what was happening yesterday is rapidly changing today and won't be recognizable tomorrow.

So, how will our twenty-first century workers behave in their workplaces? How will they use information at their fingertips to the best advantage? How will they be prepared to deal with ideas not yet conceived, decisions not yet made, and occupations not yet defined?

We in education must ensure that students see the relevance of what they are learning in school and at work today—ensure that they understand what they need to know, to value, to do in future education, training, work, and life.

Our classroom practices must reflect the workplace and present problems to be solved by teams of knowledge workers who are decision makers, effecting solutions and performing quality work.

What must educators focus on in their curricula and classrooms? I suggest fusing the following seven applied learning competencies into every activity in the classroom.

1. Communications

   - Reading

   - Writing

   - Speaking

   - Listening

   - Presenting information

   - Using a computer

2. Analysis

   - Problem solving

   - Decision making

   - Planning

3. Teamwork

4. Organizational and customer focus

5. Commitment to excellence, standards, quality, safety

6. Adaptability and continuous learning

7. Personal attributes

   - Self-confidence

   - Honesty

   - Goal orientation

   - Respect

   - Balance in work, family, school, and leisure

Quotoid

Walt Whitman: "The words of my book, nothing; the drift of it, everything."

If the teaching-learning situation focuses on these competencies, our students will be able to enter, perform, and excel in any situation presented by the workplace because they are able to respond creatively, insightfully, thoughtfully, and decisively.

Align

n these "nanosecond nineties," we are encouraged to thrive on chaos—intellectual and otherwise. Yet we are caught in a paradox: to acquire even more newly emerging data and discard no-longer-useful knowledge. Just as positions are being discarded (of the two million jobs that were lost during the 1980s, one million were management positions), so are whole industries disappearing. (For example, the typewriter industry virtually disappeared with the advent of the computer. Half the 1980 Fortune 500 companies did not appear on the 1990 list.) As individuals, as employees, as citizens, we must rethink who we are, what we know, and where we are going with what we have.

In this chapter, you are encouraged to think about your own inclinations, as well as what your management, your organization, and your industry are likely to do in the future. Understanding these will help you sift through and decide which information in the sea of knowledge is relevant and useful.

Establish Self-Importances

In Your Personal Life

This book is directed primarily at business people and the work they do in organizations, but there is more to life than work. This section begins by asking you to think about what's important in your life outside work. Complete the following exercise to get started.

Exercise:
∙∙
Assessing Personal Importances

A. Begin by thinking about ten things you would like to have more time to do, the things you would like to learn more about, the things you most enjoy, the things you feel strongly about. Include such things, if applicable, as spending more time with certain people.

1. _____

2. _____

3. _____

4. _____

5. _____

6. _____

7. _____

8. _____

9. _____

10. _____

B. Now list ten ways you spend time acquiring information. Reading the newspaper might be one, reading an electronic bulletin board another.

1. _____

2. _____

3. _____

4. _____

5. _____

6. _____

7. _____

8. _____

9. _____

10. _____

C. As you examine your second list, isolate two items that can be streamlined. A newspaper, for example, does provide important information. But you can obtain that information from radio or television, which frees you to do other things at the same time. If you enjoy reading books, you may be able to obtain the same information through printed book summaries or through audiotapes. If you scour magazines to find articles related to your interests, you could read the table of contents instead of flipping through the entire magazine.

D. Your next step is to estimate how much time you could save each week if you streamlined all you could:

_____

E. Finally, determine how you would spend this extra time. Go back to your original list and place a star beside one important item to which you would give these additional minutes or hours of your life. If you feel any hesitation whatsoever, remember that it is the time of your life. You deserve to spend it as you see fit.

In Your Professional Life

Use the process you just followed for establishing importances in your personal life to determine what you're likely to do at work. Do those inclinations reflect the importances your organization has identified? The following exercise will help you get started.

Queryoid

Who's in control?

Exercise:
Assessing Professional Importances

A. List ten things you're likely to do at work on any given day. Don't attempt to prioritize now—just jot down the first ten duties that come to mind when you think about the important elements of your job.

1. _____
2. _____
3. _____
4. _____
5. _____
6. _____
7. _____
8. _____
9. _____
10. _____

B. Now go back and write the letters "OM" beside the items that clearly support the organization's mission. If that mission hasn't been articulated, think about your manager's mission. What is it—above all else—he or she is expected to do? Place the letters "MM" beside the items that enable your manager to carry out that mission more easily.

Assessing Competencies for Jobs of the Future

Dorothy Pecoraro has identified a number of skills that she feels will be important for jobs of the future (see pp. 33-35). With those skills in mind, complete the quiz on the next page to assess your current level of expertise for each.

Quotoid

Ralph Waldo
Emerson:
"Invention
breeds
invention."

Quiz:
Assessing Skills for the Future

A. Assess your current level of expertise for each competency by placing an "X" on the continuum.

1. Communications

Reading

| Not at all proficient | Getting by | Excellent at this |

Writing

| Not at all proficient | Getting by | Excellent at this |

Speaking

| Not at all proficient | Getting by | Excellent at this |

Listening

| Not at all proficient | Getting by | Excellent at this |

Presenting information

Not at all proficient   Getting by   Excellent at this

Queryoid

Have you done your homework?

Using a computer

Not at all proficient   Getting by   Excellent at this

2. Analysis

Not at all proficient   Getting by   Excellent at this

Problem solving

Not at all proficient   Getting by   Excellent at this

Decision making

Not at all proficient   Getting by   Excellent at this

Planning

Not at all proficient   Getting by   Excellent at this

Queryoid

*Are you willing
to work hard to
escape?*

▼

3. Teamwork

Not at all   Getting by   Excellent
proficient   at this

4. Organizational and customer focus

Not at all   Getting by   Excellent
proficient   at this

5. Commitment to excellence, standards, quality, safety

Not at all   Getting by   Excellent
proficient   at this

6. Adaptability and continuous learning

Not at all   Getting by   Excellent
proficient   at this

7. Personal attributes

Self-
confidence

Not at all   Getting by   Excellent
proficient   at this

Goal
orientation

Not at all   Getting by   Excellent
proficient   at this

Balance in
work, family,
school, and
leisure

Not at all   Getting by   Excellent
proficient   at this

B. Based on what you've indicated here, what kind of
knowledge should you spend more time acquiring?

_____

_____

_____

C. What knowledge areas do you need to periodically
update?

_____

_____

_____

D. In what area do you probably already have a
sufficient amount of knowledge and so should stop
acquiring information, at least for the time being?

_____

_____

_____

Queryoid

Are you entrapped?

▼

Identify the Importances of Others

We often assume we know what's important to those around us. And yet, until we discuss their importances with them, we truly don't know what matters to them. To illustrate how far afield we often are in our assumptions about knowledge, try the exercise that begins on the next page.

Exercise:
• •
Testing Your Assumptions

A. For each item, place an "X" beside the figure you
think is most accurate.

1. How much does sexual harassment cost
organizations every year (exclusive of lawsuits, but
inclusive of absenteeism, reduced productivity, and
training)?

☐ $1 million   ☐ $3 million   ☐ $4 million
☐ $6 million   ☐ $8 million

2. How many new products are launched in America
each year?

☐ 500   ☐ 1,500   ☐ 15,000
☐ 17,000   ☐ 20,000

3. What has been the total cost of the United States'
nuclear weapons program over the last fifty years?

☐ $4 million   ☐ $14 million   ☐ $4 billion
☐ $14 billion   ☐ $4 trillion

4. How many computer companies in the world have
sales of more than one billion dollars?

☐ 15   ☐ 25   ☐ 55
☐ 75   ☐ 85   ☐ 95

5. How many of those computer companies are American companies?

☐ 10   ☐ 21   ☐ 42
☐ 59   ☐ 61   ☐ 80

6. How much do unproductive meetings cost American businesses each year?

☐ $1 billion   ☐ $11 million   ☐ $37 billion
☐ $45 million

7. How much does depression cost American firms each year?

☐ $44 million   ☐ $44 billion   ☐ $50 million
☐ $55 billion

8. How much does the average American household contribute to charity?

☐ $200   ☐ $800   ☐ $1,000
☐ $1,200

9. How many Academy Awards did Walt Disney win?

☐ 8   ☐ 11   ☐ 14
☐ 18   ☐ 23   ☐ 39
☐ 51

10. What is the largest bill the United States mint prints?

☐ $10   ☐ $50   ☐ $100
☐ $500   ☐ $1,000   ☐ $5,000

How Well Did You Do?

Check your answers below to see how many of your assumptions were correct. If some weren't, you understand how easily we can err when we assume facts. It is easy to err, too, when we assume we know how others feel.

1. $6 million
2. 17,000 new products
3. $4 trillion
4. 55 companies
5. 42 American companies

6. $37 billion
7. $44 billion
8. $800
9. 51 Academy Awards
10. $100 bill

B. Stop to consider the assumptions you make about what your boss thinks is important in each of the following areas.

1. Work priorities _____

_____

_____

_____

2. Values _____

_____

_____

_____

3. Interpersonal relations _____

_____

_____

_____

Predictoid

By the year 2200, we will need 5 million more filing cabinets than we have now.

Quotoid

*Carl Ackerman:
"Facts, when
combined with
ideas, constitute
the greatest
force in the
world."*

▼

4. Communication _____

_____

_____

C. Next, test your assumptions by asking your boss to list his or her own importances in each area and then comparing them to your own.

D. With this information in hand, you can proceed. In view of your manager's inclinations, you are now in a better position to align your efforts.

1. What information or knowledge should you be acquiring more of?

_____

_____

2. What information or knowledge should you spend less time acquiring?

_____

_____

3. What new knowledge do you need to acquire?

_____

_____

4. What shifts in your work priorities should you undertake?

_____

_____

Attend to Trends

To be sure, information has expanded beyond the capacity of a single person to absorb and understand. Because specializations exist within specializations, we must turn to experts for guidance. It is the experts who distill for us the essence of the knowledge we need, and they who prevent us from falling into black holes of information.

Let's turn to the forecasts of futurists, experts who can give us general information about what the future probably has in store for us. Knowing the way in which the nation and the world are inclining may help you formulate plans for acquiring knowledge for both yourself and your organization. Think about these forecasts from the World Future Society:

1. "Electronic immigrants" could become an international trade issue by the late 1990s. These new service workers who "telecommute" across borders via computers will perform a variety of services electronically and compete against workers in affluent countries.

2. By the year 2000, 52 percent of the world's people will reside in urban centers. That number may leap to 90 percent by the end of the twenty-first century.

3. "Copreneurs"—married couples who work together—may be the wave of America's business future. Hiring working couples as a team could be a logical step for corporations. And more married couples are expected to start their own businesses.

Queryoid

Do you look for patterns?

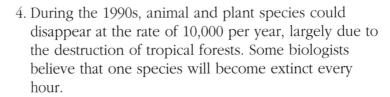

4. During the 1990s, animal and plant species could disappear at the rate of 10,000 per year, largely due to the destruction of tropical forests. Some biologists believe that one species will become extinct every hour.

5. Between now and the end of the century, the United States economy will generate $4 to $5 trillion in new capital assets, assets that will embody the next generation of applied technology. But unless current financial techniques are altered, small businesses may find access to credit even more limited in the future than they do today.

(Reprinted with permission of the World Future Society, 7910 Woodmont Avenue, Suite 450, Bethesda, MD 20814.)

Exercise:
Assessing the Impact of Trends

A. How might your industry and your life be impacted by one or more of the trends predicted by the World Future Society if they actually do come about?

_____

_____

_____

_____

_____

_____

B. In view of what you have written, what changes should you make in the way you collect, store, and retrieve information? What changes should you make in the kind of information you will need to acquire? It may help to think about this quotation by author Roger Dawson regarding Thomas Edison: "If Edison had been a CEO of a conglomerate, he probably would have insisted upon the invention of the world's best oil lantern instead of inventing the light bulb."

Before, while, or after you respond, learn what your boss thinks about the direction your organization is heading. Is your company driven to make the very

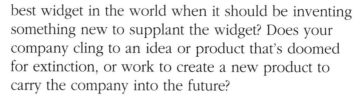

best widget in the world when it should be inventing something new to supplant the widget? Does your company cling to an idea or product that's doomed for extinction, or work to create a new product to carry the company into the future?

You may wish to demonstrate your leadership skills by forming a team to investigate national and industry trends and to contemplate how best to prepare for them.

Summary

Yes, you may find data, data everywhere and not a drop of knowledge to drink. Finding time to wade through the ever-widening waters of information in order to isolate droplets of significance becomes more difficult each day. The only solution is to make choices—and those choices must be guided by external forces. What trends are emerging in our personal and professional lives? Thinking about trends and the technology available in the culture of convenience will help you choose the data most relevant to your life and work style.

Investigating your own inclinations, as well as those of your management, organization, and industry can help you make intelligent choices. *Knowing* what is important to your boss, for example, rather than *assuming* what is important, enables you to achieve congruence between your efforts and his or her expectations. In this quality-driven era, organizations may have to rethink choices too. Should world-class quality in existing products be the aim, or should resources be directed to creating a whole new product? (Remember that if Edison had sought to perfect the oil lantern, he probably would never have invented the light bulb.)

If you're like most people, time is a rare commodity. You must, therefore, seek better ways to control how you use it. One such way is to make technology work for you. If you regard your job as a series of tasks to be accomplished rather than as a number of hours to be spent in one location, you can rethink how and where to

Quotoid

Proverb: "Lose an hour in the morning and you'll be hunting for it all day."

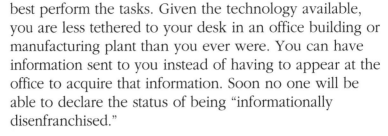

Queryoid

*To what extent
are your
company's
managers
opening the
books?*

▼

best perform the tasks. Given the technology available, you are less tethered to your desk in an office building or manufacturing plant than you ever were. You can have information sent to you instead of having to appear at the office to acquire that information. Soon no one will be able to declare the status of being "informationally disenfranchised."

Clearly communicating with your manager will allow you to use electronic tools to increase your productivity. Choosing your own time and space to carry out tasks is usually advantageous for you, your manager, and your organization. But these decisions—as well as decisions about which tasks should be done—are never made in a vacuum. They begin with information input, are shaped by introspection, and are ultimately executed via numerous assumption-busting exchanges with your boss. If you are to align your importances with the importances of others, you need to speak up, hear and be heard.

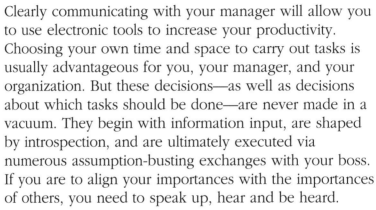

Interview with Karen Tongias Panzeri, Executive Director of Marketing, Whitehall (assisted living, rehabilitation and nursing care center) Boca Raton, Florida

Queryoid

Is your team freed by or fettered by information?

As an executive director of marketing, I have many projects floating all day long and all through each month. I attend regular meetings of the Chamber of Commerce; Soroptimist's International, for which I am the current president; Professional Resources Network; and the Association for Professional Saleswomen. I also attend meetings for the Alzheimer's, cancer, stroke, and heart associations. You can surmise that I receive numerous newsletters, articles, and other information from all of these.

I usually take action by writing important dates in my calendar. When I learn about new information in my industry, I don't memorize it. Rather, I know who my resources are and my contacts. So, when I need to use the information, I know where to find it again.

When important seminars are offered, I usually block time off to attend. I maintain a marketing calendar and schedule different events, much as I do with my regular appointments. In this way, I am assured that I accomplish the marketing goals I have set.

My day-to-day activities involve giving information out to families by phone or by personal interview. During these stressful family crisis situations, I must remain unshaken so I can help the family with the process of making difficult decisions.

I think the best way to keep the totality of information in perspective, without feeling inundated, especially in the highly regulated business of nursing homes, is to know where to locate the sources of that information through a network of contacts and resources built up over the years.

Streamline

To assimilate the voluminous amounts of knowledge that bombard us, you must find shortcuts. If you don't, you will find yourself suffering from the Information Age malady known as Info-Angst—an anxiety caused by the feeling that there's too much to absorb, too much to accomplish, and too little time in which to do it.

Many professionals experience a natural rush toward information. They are driven to acquire more and more intellectual wealth. As John Sculley, former CEO of Apple Computers, has noted: "The Information Age is a revolution. It's a revolution that's global in scope, with few safe harbors for isolationists."

Obviously, to remain competitive professionally, you must remain current not with all the data that can be

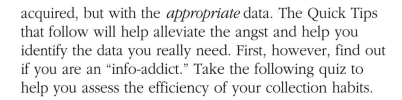

Queryoid

Are you ruthless with time?

▼

acquired, but with the *appropriate* data. The Quick Tips that follow will help alleviate the angst and help you identify the data you really need. First, however, find out if you are an "info-addict." Take the following quiz to help you assess the efficiency of your collection habits.

Quiz:
••
Are You an "Info-Addict"?

Answer "yes" or "no" to each item.

Yes   No

☐   ☐   1. I enjoy reading about many different subjects.

☐   ☐   2. I keep extensive files.

☐   ☐   3. I can find any filed paper I need within five minutes.

☐   ☐   4. I can locate anything on my desk in seconds.

☐   ☐   5. I find the info-access capability of computers exciting.

☐   ☐   6. When I find information that will be of interest to colleagues, I cut it out (or make a copy) and send it to them.

☐   ☐   7. I have many cross-references in my files.

☐   ☐   8. If I am out of the office for a prolonged time, others can easily find what they need in my files.

☐   ☐   9. I have a voracious appetite for new knowledge.

☐   ☐   10. I have files I have not referred to for more than six months.

What it all means:

Give yourself ten points for "yes" answers to the questions 1, 2, 3, 4, 5, 7, 8, 9 and ten points for "no" answers to questions 6 and 10.

If you scored 80 or higher, you are ready for the Info-Olympics! You enjoy swimming in a sea of knowledge but have learned to control the waves of information. If you scored 80 or less, the following three techniques may help you.

1. Avoid the temptation to become a clipping service for the numerous other info-addicts you know. While there is nothing wrong with occasionally sending your architect brother-in-law an article about Frank Lloyd Wright, if you engage in such actions frequently, you are letting information control you.

2. Keep your files updated. Even if it's only once a year, periodically purge—and encourage others to do the same.

3. If you have misplaced a paper, rather than stopping what you are doing to find it (assuming you do not need it immediately), add it to a "lost list" and look for it later.

Streamlining Quick Tips

Streamlining in the Information Age involves being selective about which ideas and information you will pay attention to and assimilate. It also entails managing your time in order to manage the tasks that evolve from the abundance of information (e.g., writing/reading reports, making presentations, attending meetings, etc.). The following quick tips will help you in these areas.

Quick Tips for Assimilating Information

A tidal wave of information washes over you every day. Which ideas and information should you try to channel? Which can you direct into meaningful knowledge?

One excellent means of gaining quick access to the knowledge you need is to scan documents to determine what to do with them. Is it junk mail? Throw it out. Could someone else profit from it more than you? Pass it along. Is it information you need for the future? File it. Is it information you need for a current project? Read it now. Keep a stack of new file folders ready so you can properly sort the incoming information as it arrives on your desk.

Here's another technique you can use with information that's valuable but not critical (such as books related to your field of interest, magazine articles, and the daily newspaper): Read only the first sentence in each paragraph. Ninety percent of such paragraphs contain the main idea right in the first sentence. So, if you're pressed for time, you can glean a good understanding of the article by merely absorbing the opening sentences of each paragraph.

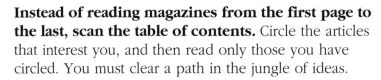

Instead of reading magazines from the first page to the last, scan the table of contents. Circle the articles that interest you, and then read only those you have circled. You must clear a path in the jungle of ideas.

You can use the same technique when viewing television. Instead of channel-surfing to avoid the least-boring programs, read the television guide and decide in advance which one or two programs are truly worth your time.

Although too much information can create Info-Angst, so too can too little information. If, for example, you don't have enough information about what's expected of you or of your team, you may be laboring under unnecessary stress. Make a list of all your questions at the beginning of a new project. Then meet with your boss or your team advisor and get the clarification you need.

If others abuse your e-mail, ask them to limit the input to truly important messages. Similarly, if you receive more junk mail than you would like, contact the senders and ask them to remove your name from their mailing lists. To easily do so, type a simple message on blank address labels and affix them and a 20-cent stamp to a pile of postcards. Then, when more junk mail arrives, you need only to add the address of the sender and mail it. Or you could drop a note to the following service:

Mail List Removal Service
P.O. Box 9008
Farmingdale, NY 11735

Think of consolidation possibilities. Be inspired by this 1996 Budget Resolution from the House of Representatives:

> "Consolidate the Bureau of the Census and the Bureau of Economic Analysis into an independent U.S. statistical administration. U.S. government statistics are collected and analyzed by at least 25 federal offices, departments and agencies; each constructs indices differently, uses different time periods and different base years. There is no central organization setting standards for the quality of consistency. Consequently, many statistics compiled by the U.S. government are suspect. This proposal calls for consolidating many of the statistical organizations in the U.S. government with the Census Bureau to achieve qualitative improvement and efficiencies."

Learn to transform obese input to bare-bones output—and insist that others do the same. Some organizations are so insistent on being Info-Floaters and not Info-Floodeds that they require all internal communications to be pared down. To illustrate, in some companies, employees who wish to have a meeting with a manager and are unable to state the purpose of the meeting on the back of a business card are not granted the manager's time. Similarly, other organizations require that employees limit all memos to one page.

The following exercise is designed to test your skill at whittling away excess verbiage.

Factoid

Fifty-one percent of Americans feel they don't have time enough to do everything they want to do."

Exercise:
Getting to the Point

Below is an "obese input"—one where information is unnecessarily verbose. Condense it to a "bare-bones output"—a message that can fit on the back of a business card. Note your starting time here: _____

Input

There is a growing number of knowledgeable experts who are of the opinion that an urgency exists in terms of the need for businesses to fully utilize digital technology. More than a decade ago, a number of forward-thinking companies such as Wal-Mart Stores Inc. were able to become world-class competitors by way of the use of networks to support creative and innovative approaches to the way they do business. In the vernacular, the full utilization of these digital transmissions capabilities is called "getting wired."

The necessity for making full use of electronic communications is clear, as are the benefits: to expedite internal processes and to widen the customer base. If a company is indeed wired, it will be able to eliminate the factors that often prevent growth. Among those factors are temporal and spatial considerations.

Output

Write your bare-bones version of the previous message here.

_____

_____

_____

_____

_____

_____

_____

Is your message similar to the following?

"Our company should be thinking about electronic commerce."

Ending time: _____

Queryoid

Do you think about what not to put in?

Quick Tips for Optimizing Time

Managing your time involves distinguishing which tasks are the "vital few" and which are the "trivial many." Does this sound familiar?

A supervisor began a new work week determined to get through the mountain of paperwork stacked on his desk. He picked up the first item on the stack, a memo from his manager, and dutifully began reading it. He noted that his manager needed figures for a variance report and went to the files to find them. While going through the files, he came across a letter from an angry customer that he thought he could cite in a presentation he and his team had to make for the Quality Council. That made him think about the date for the presentation and he left the files to check his calendar. As he was doing so, the phone rang. It was a supervisor in another department asking for data on a recent printing job. The supervisor told the caller he would get right back to him and returned to the files to find the data. He soon located it, along with notes he had made to himself about improving similar print runs in the future. He wanted to take care of the print-data interruption immediately, but he realized he had not taken down the extension number for the other supervisor. He called the switchboard operator to learn what it was and remembered to ask her about her son's surgery. After learning a great deal about ulna fractures, he dialed his colleague and gave him the data. The supervisor got right back to work but was soon interrupted by an employee asking about the upcoming celebration the department was planning for having worked 100,000 hours without a single accident. After several minutes of verbal backslapping, the supervisor went to his desk to locate the notice about the celebration. After a few minutes, he found it and—when the employee asked to have a copy—the manager willingly obliged. When he returned from the copy machine, he gave the employee a copy and returned to his desk, determined to continue making progress with the paper mountain. To his horror, he realized he was still on the same memo ... and a full hour was gone from the morning he had begun with best intentions.

The point is this: If you truly wish to reach the top of the paper mountain and happily descend the other side, you must exert self-discipline. Here are some tips for doing so.

Time managers swear by a time log to keep track of their daily activities. It's an easy way to track how you spend your time at work. To assess your time management skills, use the chart provided on the next page or create your own by writing down all your daily activities across the top of a piece of paper. Divide your working hours into half-hour segments vertically down the left side of the page. Make ten copies of this chart to keep track of two weeks' worth of activities. Every ten minutes during the day, place a check mark to indicate which activity you have been working on.

Factoid

Six weeks are lost each year by executives looking for misplaced information.

	Phone	Meeting	Paper work	Site visit	Read	Breaks
8:00	✔		✔			✔
8:30						
9:00						
9:30						
10:00						
10:30						
11:00						
11:30						
12:00						
12:30						
1:00						
1:30						
2:00						
2:30						
3:00						
3:30						
4:00						
4:30						
5:00						

After two weeks, assess how you are spending your time and make changes accordingly.

Keep a "to do" list for both long-range and short-range projects. Doing so will keep you current and enable you to keep track of deadlines. Prioritize your lists in any manner that works for you: alphabetical, numerated, or even color-coded. (The originator of the "to do" list, consultant Ivy Lee, earned $10,000 for devising this simple but effective means of self-organization.)

Determine when your "prime time" is. During what part of a typical work day do you operate at peak performance? Schedule for that period the tasks:

- You find most challenging.

- You dislike most.

- That are most important.

- That require you to convert information to knowledge.

Information doesn't exist in a vacuum. As stated throughout this book, it is a means by which knowledge is produced. When you analyze raw data, for example, you transform those data into a report you and/or others can use to make a decision. The information almost always has deadlines associated with it. To keep a step ahead of all those deadlines, make note of each one you're accountable for and place the notes in a tickler file. A tickler file is simply an accordion folder or a set of file folders, one for each day of the month. Place your deadline reminders in a folder several days ahead of each actual deadline, so it doesn't creep up on you at the last minute.

Quotoid

Anonymous: "Always put off until tomorrow what you shouldn't do at all."

Factoid

The annual sales of over-the-counter pain relievers has increased in the last decade by $500 million.

Quick Tips for Managing Multiple Priorities

As the previous vignette about the supervisor illustrated, we often must deal with multiple tasks of pressing importance. Here are some ways to manage your tasks when several are competing for your time and attention simultaneously.

Keep a record of "lessons learned" for each project you undertake. Refer to it the next time you have a similar project.

Schedule some interruption-free time every day. You can also use it as contingency time should something go wrong.

Know that work expands to the amount of time you allocate to it. (It's called "Parkinson's Law.") Develop a sense of what-can-be-done-by-when and work to realize your time estimates.

Develop a checklist for each priority item. The checklist should include the necessary steps for accomplishing each task, including the approvals required. Keeping these checklists will ensure that nothing gets overlooked.

Prioritize. When your day seems all too hectic, return to a solid foundation by quickly determining what has to be dealt with now and what can be postponed (but not forgotten).

Find shortcuts. Ask if this work, or something similar, has been done before. Check with people inside and outside the organization.

Tools and Strategies

Besides the suggestions presented in the Quick Tips, try incorporating some of these more "meaty" information management strategies into your routine.

Stratification

As noted, the Information Age has spawned a whole set of tasks, routines, and responsibilities concerned with the handling and management of data. It's also generated new tasks and responsibilities that involve using information to create knowledge and new ideas. The stratification technique is helpful for assigning priorities to these tasks.

When you stratify, you examine a number of seemingly unrelated items or chunks of knowledge to determine whether there are patterns or common threads among them. The stratifying technique is useful for those who feel waves of responsibility continuously washing over them.

Begin by listing all your current responsibilities at work and at home. Don't include actions such as "answer the phone when it rings," but rather unfinished work or incomplete projects.

Once you've created your list, "stratify" it. In other words, what large categories seem to emerge? For each category you think of, write the following information at the top of a clean sheet of paper.

- Category
- Ultimate completion date

- Input needed from
- Priority number

Next, prioritize the categories. To complete this step, you will need to consider a number of factors—the importance your boss gives it, the time element, the cost, your interest, and so on.

Finally, transfer every item on the original list to the new sheets in prioritized order.

Getting a handle on the work you have to do won't lessen the work itself, but it will lessen the amount of anxiety you experience when you think about those responsibilities.

Apply the Must/May Approach

The Must/May Approach is another useful way to sort out the conflicting demands on the time in your day. Begin each morning or the end of each day by drawing a box like the following:

	Must	**May**
Do		
Call		

In the appropriate boxes, list the things you must do and the calls you must make. Also list the things you may get done, and the calls you may make, depending on the time factor. The procedure is a simple but effective one, especially if you keep the box in a prominent place.

Use the 2-2-2-2 Technique

Patients who suffer with back problems frequently use an exercise program known as 2-2-2 (for spondylolisthesis stabilization). For 2 minutes, 2 times a day, the patient uses an object 2 inches high to exercise. The same technique can be used to manage your files and the information they contain.

Make 2 piles of the things you must get done, the reports you must read, the memos you must respond to, and so on. The piles shouldn't be higher than 2 inches. Then, 2 times a day for at least 2 minutes each time, attack the work (alternate the piles). You can quit after 2 minutes, but typically you will find that having started, you don't mind finishing at least one of the projects in the pile.

Take the "Ow" Out of "Now"

This idea for tackling paperwork is based on reward. You will need to work with a colleague to carry it out.

First, both you and your colleague, working independently, should list one reward on each of fifteen small sheets of paper. The rewards can be pay-offs such as the following:

- "Lift up your wastepaper basket. You will find a candy bar beneath it."

Predictoid

By the year 2000, there will be 1 million journals in print.

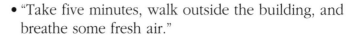
- "Take five minutes, walk outside the building, and breathe some fresh air."

- "Here is fifty cents. Go to the vending machines, and buy yourself a cup of coffee. You deserve it."

- "Open the attached envelope and read the funny stories inside it for the next few minutes."

- "Call Jim Smith at extension 23. He has something nice to tell you."

Be creative in your reward gestures. They need not be expensive, but they should be thoughtful enough to help you and your colleague overcome the urge to procrastinate paperwork.

Next, fold up the papers and exchange them. Paper clip one folded-up sheet to each of the difficult or unappealing paperwork tasks you need to complete this week. After you complete a given task, unfold the paper and indulge yourself.

Summary

Admittedly, being alive in the Information Age means being challenged by ideas moment by moment. What can be more exhilarating than to gain answers to questions with a mere push of a button? But the sheer volume of answers can create anxiety as well. This chapter provided Quick Tips for assimilating information, optimizing time, reducing Info-Angst, and managing multiple priorities.

It also provided these more ambitious strategies:

- *Stratification* requires listing all your uncompleted tasks and then stratifying the list. You should allocate one full page for each category of responsibility.

- *The Must/May Approach* is best used at the end of the day to prepare for the following day, or at the beginning of a new day. This approach asks you to divide all your tasks into those that you *must* do for a given day and those you *may* get done, depending on time that may be available.

- *The 2-2-2-2 Technique* asks you to devote at least 2 minutes, 2 times a day, to working on assignments in one of 2 stacks of least-favored work, with each stack no higher than 2 inches.

- *Taking the "Ow" Out of "Now" Reward System* requires cooperating with a friend who will describe rewards on small sheets of paper. When you have completed a particularly unpleasant task, you open the folded note to find your reward.

Queryoid

How do you reward yourself for getting things done?

As beneficial as these ideas are, they work only if you work. If you aren't improving your techniques for streamlining and remaining afloat, you will soon be going under. As much as you may wish to stop the wave of information, you can't. The only way to survive and perhaps even thrive is to continuously improve your skills. Strive to streamline the data you have to deal with by knowing which you should pay attention to and which you can ignore. Then employ methods for streamlining the tasks that result from the information—learn to manage your time and set priorities.

Interview with Jonathan Rintels, screenwriter, "Snowbound: The Jim & Jennifer Stopa Story" (CBS)

Queryoid

Do you save everything?

I've learned to be very selective. I judge carefully the kinds of information that come along. The choices are often difficult, but they have to be made. For example, I recall when I used a computer to connect with other members of the Writers Guild. Communicating this way soon became addictive for me. I found that I was commenting on a thread of an idea and then responding to the response to my comment, and then responding to the response to the response. I finally had to cut it out completely. I couldn't get any writing done!

As expansive as America Online is, I quit using that as well. It was a novelty, a toy, but it was not really aiding me in my research. It took more time for me to read about all the possibilities, decide which to download, print them, and then read the printouts than it would have taken to simply drive to the library and pick up a few books or articles. Besides, I like the ambiance of the library more than I like the Internet's.

To stay abreast of all that's happening, I'm devoted to CNN because of the immediacy of the news it provides. By the time I finish reading an article in the *Washington Post*, the situation could have changed radically. Print-media news is outdated very quickly, but CNN provides accurate, up-to-the-minute news on a variety of subjects. I keep it on in the background while I'm reading or doing something else. I also try to listen to books on audiotape when I drive.

Quotoid

Jose Ortega Y Gasset:
"Thinking is the endeavor to capture reality by means of ideas."

We can be swept away with the novelty of electronic tools and toys. I need to be computer literate, of course, but I find "traditional" literacy is more useful.

In our rush to embrace the new, we cannot totally discard the old means of accessing and using information.

4

Refine

You're at the halfway point in this book now—a good time to review, reflect, and refine. This book began by emphasizing the need to make choices. That emphasis will continue—you will be asked to choose among all the tips and techniques you have been given and begin a plan of action. First, though, let's review.

To begin, you "defined." You diagnosed yourself, your team, your organization to determine whether you are floundering or swimming briskly in the sea of information. Next you "aligned." You learned what pursuits are important to you and to your organization. You were encouraged to consider the direction your industry as a whole seems to be inclining towards in view of events predicted by futurists. The "streamline" chapter provided a number of techniques for assimilating information, optimizing your time, and managing multiple priorities.

In this chapter, you will "refine." You will reexamine your priorities and define them even further. Prompts are provided to aid you in formulating an action plan.

The REFINE method, in particular, allows you to play leapfrog over the stacks of information piling up everywhere you look. Here are its basic elements:

Reassess

Enlighten

Find a workable plan

Integrate

Network

Energize

Read on to find out how to plan your strategy for better using information.

Reassess

Review the exercises you completed in previous chapters. Skim them for the things you learned about yourself. In view of everything presented thus far, reassess your information goals, keeping in mind how data is processed:

- Information is acquired.

- Information is stored.

- Information is recalled.

- Information is applied.

Using this model, formulate an actual plan for achieving your information goals. Answering the questions in the following exercise will help you plot out your plan.

Factoid

Information doubles every five years.

Developing a Plan

1. Write down one thing you can do to improve the way you acquire information.

   _____

   _____

   _____

2. What is one thing you can do to improve the way you mentally store data?

   _____

   _____

   _____

3. What is one thing you can do to improve your recall of the information you have stored?

   _____

   _____

   _____

4. What is one thing you can do to improve the way you use information?

   _____

   _____

   _____

After answering these questions, consider the following:

- Will these decisions, this plan, still be relevant a year from now?

- Can I set deadlines and stick to them?

- Do I need assistance in setting/sticking to this plan?

- Am I willing to keep evaluating my progress periodically?

- Am I a continuous learner?

Enlighten

The Enlighten component of the REFINE strategy asks you to enlighten yourself and ultimately others about ways to efficiently absorb information. The following is one especially profitable technique that involves the use of a skeletal image.

It works like this. Before you begin to assimilate a body of information, whether it is visually or verbally presented, imagine a skeleton that represents the information you're about to receive. Divide the skeleton into five parts, reflecting the head and four limbs. The skeleton will serve as the outline for your information. As you think about the body of information in its totality, think, too, about the major divisions. Then, as you begin to  absorb information, place it in one of the five skeletal categories. Using the skeletal outline will enhance your proficiency not only in the information-intake stage but also in the storage and retrieval stages.

Find a Workable Plan

Factoid

By the year 2000, the amount of information available will double every 20 months.

Goal-setting is a matter of looking at your life (personal and/or professional parts of it) from a long-range perspective. Individually, organizationally, nationally, we lose the opportunity to take advantage of events if we have not prepared for their eventuality. The process is difficult in a sense because it forces us to think about what we want from life—and the average person hasn't done so. As difficult as the process is, however, it is worth undertaking because it gives us a sense of control over our lives. It also increases the likelihood that the things we value will come into our lives. In essence, we have to set aside time to plan, write down our goals, periodically check to see if we are meeting the milestones, celebrate our successes, and then set new goals.

Thus far, you've examined only parts of the action plan. Now answer specific, sequential questions that will result in a comprehensive, concrete plan for you to follow. You have reassessed your intentions as a result of having read half the book. You have enlightened yourself by learning about the skeletal strategy. Now, plan the work and work the plan by answering the following questions:

1. In terms of acquiring and using information more efficiently, what is a realistic short-range goal you could set and achieve?

   _____

   _____

   _____

Queryoid

What percentage of your brain are you using?

▼

2. What is a realistic long-range goal?

_____

_____

_____

3. What skills would someone who is outstanding in the acquisition and use of information possess? (It may help to think of someone you know who is exemplary in this regard.)

_____

_____

_____

_____

_____

4. Match your skills to the skills of the person you listed in question 3.

_____

_____

_____

_____

_____

5. In view of the comparison, what skills do you need to improve or acquire?

_____

_____

_____

6. Where can you go and what can you do to obtain the improvement you need?

Queryoid

What do you take away from the training you attend?

◄

_____

_____

_____

_____

_____

7. List all the costs (financial, physical, time, familial, emotional, etc.) associated with the improvement you plan to seek.

_____

_____

_____

_____

_____

8. How can you reduce those costs?

_____

_____

_____

_____

9. Whom will you call upon to assist you? When?

_____

_____

_____

10. What is the time frame for both your short-term and your long-term goals?

_____

_____

_____

_____

11. How will you remind yourself of what your goals are?

_____

_____

_____

_____

_____

_____

There's no trick to being successful at goal setting. The real trick is believing you are capable of realizing the goals you have set. Dream of being the person you wish to become. And remember, "Nothing is as real as a dream."

Integrate

Integrating refers to putting your plan into action—as quickly and as painlessly as possible. Quickness is the thrust behind Professor George Zipf's famous Law. In short, it says we use abbreviations (USA) instead of unnecessarily articulating full references (United States of America). Obeying his law, expend the least amount of effort possible as you integrate your thoughts about your action plan. One way to do this is to use the L-I-F-T model.

1. **List everything you plan to do or would like to do to deal more proficiently with the information deluging your life.** Consider how massive the deluge is: There was more information produced between 1965 and 1995 than was produced in the 5,000-year time span from 3000 B.C. to 1965.

2. **Interlink that information.** Cross out duplicates. Combine two similar items. Subsume some information into larger categories. Find connections and use them to reduce your efforts.

3. **Funnel the many specifics down into one broad, well-defined statement of what you will do to cope with Information Overload.** Let this statement be the distilled essence of all your plans and intended efforts.

4. **Test the plan.** Discard what isn't working. Keep what is. Make revisions as needed. Put the amended plan into action. List - Interlink - Funnel - Test. It will work for you if you put it to work.

Quotoid

Stephen Wright: "You can't have everything. Where would you put it?"

Another means of eliminating duplication and integrating efforts is to prepare a flow diagram. What is the flow of the work? Where are the bottlenecks? Where is the work being duplicated? Where are most of the errors occurring? Where is most of the time being spent? The flow diagram is relatively easy to produce. It begins with an oval representing the input that begins a work process. It ends, too, with an oval that depicts the output—the product that is passed on to the next person in the work sequence. In between are rectangles to reflect the actual steps in the process and diamonds to reflect decision points—questions answerable by "yes" or "no."

Concerning the sample flow diagram on the next page, questions that might naturally arise and for which data would need to be gathered include the following:

- How often do we have to return the requests?

- Why are they being returned?

- What can we do to ensure they are prepared correctly?

- How much time is wasted when requests have to be sent through the system again?

- Is there a better way to process purchase orders?

- If we were to redesign the process from scratch, what would it look like?

Integration is both a centrifugal and a centripetal force. *Centrifugal* force moves away from the center. A centrifugal analysis would be the flow diagram, which you would use to examine a central process by asking questions that radiate outward, away from that core.

Sample Flow Diagram

Process: Preparing a purchase order

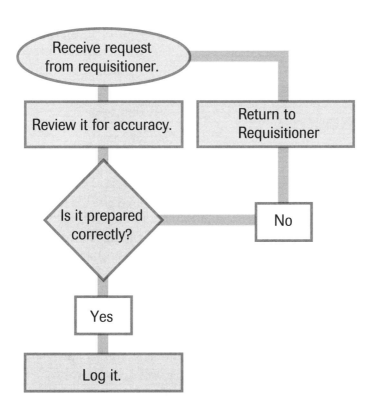

Quotoid

*Randall Tobias:
"If we had a
similar progress
in automotive
technology
(compared to
computer
technology),
today you could
buy a Lexus for
about $2. It
would travel at
the speed of
sound, and go
about 600 miles
on a thimble of
gas."*

Centripetal force moves toward the center. When you integrate by reducing overlap, by combining similar efforts, by eliminating the unnecessary, you seek to determine the essence and to pull critical elements toward the center.

Whether centrifugal or centripetal, you must analyze your information; otherwise, you can make no selections. And without selection, you are doomed to drown in ever-escalating waves of information.

Network

Your action plan has a better chance of succeeding if you subscribe to the 3-S foundation of networking.

1. **Support.** In what ways will you support your own efforts to keep information under control? (Revise your filing system, for example.) In what ways can you elicit the support of others? (Ask that your name be taken off routing lists, for example.)

2. **Share information.** What information do you have that could be passed to others? What information do others have that you can access to make your job easier? Who will make it unnecessary for wheels to be reinvented? If someone isn't willing to share that information, what other means (including electronic) could you use to obtain what you need? (Note that 96 percent of respondents in a recent *Inc.* magazine survey reported that they have increased productivity as a result of technology.)

3. **Substitute.** Think about who or what (a tape recorder, perhaps) can substitute for you at meetings. Think about who can do some of your reading. (Can an assistant scan professional journals for you and mark articles related to topics you have identified as important?) What substitutions can you make in the way you usually acquire information? (Instead of reading the paper, can you listen to the news while you're doing something else?)

Energize

You may be so swamped with paperwork and overloaded with information that you are a prisoner of numbers and words. Can you break free? Yes. And when you do, you will have more time, and more energy. Use them well.

Who jails us in the metaphorical prison? We do it to ourselves. Co-workers do it to us. Those we manage and supervisors do as well. You will have to take the initiative and request that you be excused from meetings to which you have nothing to contribute. Advise others that you already have enough information on a particular topic and that you wish no more for the time being. Stop buying books. Cancel some of your magazine subscriptions. Spend less time on the Internet. Ask your supervisor whether all the reports you prepare are really necessary or whether some of them can be abbreviated.

These are but a few of the ways you can limit your intake of information—as tempting as it might be to dive in and drown yourself with the minutiae-droplets that constitute Info-Flood.

Factoid

Use of the World Wide Web system increased 1,713 percent from 1993 to 1994.

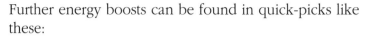

Further energy boosts can be found in quick-picks like these:

- When you make a breakthrough in reducing your information intake, reward yourself, if only by bragging to a co-worker.

- Eat an energizing food, such as fruit—an excellent energy source. (Complex carbohydrates—breads, grains, and beans—are ideal sources of long-lasting energy.)

- Clear your head if you've been working too intensely. Take a walk around the building before resuming your intense concentration.

- Do ten quick stretches. Then tackle that tough job again.

- Switch jobs. If you've been working with columns of numbers, try working with page layout. If you have been writing, clean out a desk drawer or make a phone call.

- Give yourself a break. Go to the lunch room and chat with a co-worker.

Summary

In this chapter, you refined the tentative plans you've made so far, in terms of developing a strategy for coping with Info-Flood.

The acronym R-E-F-I-N-E assists in developing an action plan:

Reassess

Enlighten

Find an action plan

Integrate

Network

Energize

To begin, reassess your goals regarding information, particularly as they parallel cognitive processes: acquiring knowledge, storing it, recalling it, and applying it. Enlighten yourself by learning how to be more efficient in your information usage. One useful technique is the skeletal strategy, which you can use to develop categories for outlining information you are about to receive.

Next, find a workable plan. This requires identifying both short- and long-range goals and the skills you need to obtain those goals. Also consider the various costs associated with acquiring the skills in order to reach the goals. It is incumbent on planners to seek ways to reduce those costs.

Factoid

The amount of electronic mail has increased 3,000 percent in the past ten years.

Predictoid

By the year 2000, less than 50 percent of the global industrial work force will have full-time jobs inside organizations.

▼

Integration uses another acronym: L-I-F-T.

- **L**ist everything you plan to do.

- **I**nterlink by categorizing, by getting a handle on the items in the list.

- **F**unnel into a single, simplified statement the outline of the plan. Such funneling is often facilitated by using a flow diagram and asking probing questions about what the diagram reveals. The creation of the statement of intent requires looking at the information flow from both a centrifugal and a centripetal perspective.

- **T**est the plan and make adjustments as needed.

The next step is to network. The 3-S approach will assist here. It requires you to think of who or what can support you as you work to implement your plan, to think of whom you can share information with and vice versa, and to think of who or what can be substituted in your acquisition and usage of data.

Finally, you must energize yourself (and others). It may help to think of breaking free from the paperwork prison. One strategy is to narrow your focus. Another is to improve your files. The third is to become proactive in limiting the amount of information being sent your way.

Interview with Chris Hunter, Vice President, Human Resource Development (HRD) Press, Amherst, Massachusetts

Given my job, the three newspapers I read, the weekly magazines and professional journals to which I subscribe—I find a great deal of my time is spent acquiring and assimilating information. To keep it all in order, I maintain two different files—one for general information, and the other for technical or job-related information. As soon as I find something of interest in the paper or in a magazine, I immediately cut it out and put it in one of these two files. If I wait, hoping to do it later, I will not be able to find it. Even at this crude level of differentiation, I can always find want I want.

Further, I always carry a large notebook with me. It has all the phone and callback information I need. In just one book, I can locate what I need no matter where I am, even without access to a Rolodex. If you use this system, make certain you date each entry so you'll have a record.

I make full use of my desk calendar too. If I see a notice of a meeting or conference, I write it down. Then, with a quick glance, I can see what's coming up and plan accordingly.

The final organizational technique that keeps me from succumbing to the glut of information I'm exposed to daily is a file of new projects and ideas. That file is

Factoid

In 1993, one-tenth of surveyed companies planned to have a data warehouse. Today, the figure is more than 90 percent.

getting bigger and bigger. However, no matter what I need to retrieve, I can find it in one of those three files: general, technical, and new. So, all incoming data is subjugated to this filing system. Of course, I have separate files on each of our authors, but that is standard.

If I find something of interest to others, I fax it to them right away so I do not have to feel responsible for keeping information that might be important to the organization. I don't like being in the position of saying: "Gee, I read something about that. Now let me see if I can find it in my files."

Final thoughts: To relive the general stress of information, I cover a lot without necessarily reading thoroughly. I focus on what is really important. I try to be selective. And, of course, I purge all my files about twice a year.

5

Confine

Armed with an action plan—the life jacket that will keep you afloat—you are now in a better position to make decisions about what information you need to confine, or limit, and how to do so.

Information fascinates us. But if we don't control the fascination, it will serve as a detriment to other, perhaps more important, obligations in our lives. A case in point is an article from the *Rochester Review* (Fall 1995, p. 8) in which a researcher noted a steady drop in grades among good college students. It turns out that these students had begun communicating on-line and had become "addicted."

Factoid

The amount of paper circulating in offices in the United States grows twice as fast as the gross national product.

This chapter discusses specific means for confining the amount of data you allow into your life:

- Being a strict time manager is one way to confine the information you encounter and must deal with each day. For example, limiting your on-line use to thirty minutes and your journal reading to one hour each day confines these "information-gathering" activities so that you'll have time to complete other tasks.

- Being able to manage meetings is a key way to confine information. Much of what is presented at meetings is tangential, unnecessary information. In fact, many times meetings aren't even needed, and resources are wasted by having them.

- Being able to confine energy and effort to the most positive and productive results should be a major organizational goal. One of the ways to do this is to make training of employees a regular routine. But the information/knowledge that's learned in the classroom must also be transferred to the workplace or job site.

- Acquiring new knowledge/information results in change of some sort—in processes, in schedules, in products, and so on. In other words, change is inevitable in the Information Age. Confining the amount of time and energy spent resisting and, instead, finding ways to smooth the transition are essential to survival.

In this chapter, each of these will be examined in turn. But first take the following quiz to see where you need to work on confining.

Exercise:
······································
Identifying "Confinement" Weaknesses

Yes   **No**

☐   ☐   1. Do you have more than one inch worth of filing to do?

☐   ☐   2. Do you waste time looking for lost items?

☐   ☐   3. Do you subscribe to more than one newspaper?

☐   ☐   4. Do you feel you have more work than time to do it in?

☐   ☐   5. Do you worry about work when you're away from it?

☐   ☐   6. Do you ever dream about not finishing a task?

☐   ☐   7. Do you notice that others get more done than you do?

☐   ☐   8. Do you only read work-related material?

☐   ☐   9. Do you feel guilty when you're on the Internet?

☐   ☐   10. Are your bookshelves sagging from the weight of books?

Interpret your score:

How many "no" answers did you have?

0: You clearly control, confine, and set clear goals for what has to be done and how much time should be allocated to it.

1-3: Heads up! You may be on your way to becoming a drowning victim. You already have a good sense of what needs to be done. Just keep on doing what you're doing, but try an occasional improvement idea.

4+: Help is on the way. Read the remainder of this chapter and pledge to put at least one suggestion to work immediately.

Manage Your Work

A study of 1,000 business executives conducted by consultant Roger Flax found that the inability to manage time was one of the top three complaints bosses had about the people they manage or supervise. (The inability to solve problems and poor writing skills were the other two.)

In its most basic sense, time management is a question of confining your desires within the fence of available resources. Those who truly manage time assess what they want to get done in a given time, allocate chunks of time for getting it done, and manage—more often than not—to accomplish their intentions. But time management takes practice and it takes assessment. Here are some tips for better estimating the time you will need to get specific things done:

- **For your next project, estimate how long it will take you to complete it.** Compare your actual completion time to the estimate. The more you do of this, the closer you will come to "getting a feel" for how long things will take.

- **Place an alarm clock on your desk.** Set it to go off at the time you expect to have a job completed. Knowing you have an audible deadline will help keep you focused.

- **Put a limit on conversations—and stick to it.** The next time someone asks, "Got a minute?" state that you have three but that you have important work to get back to after that time.

Queryoid

How would you describe your meetings?

▼

- **Make time to do "double duty."** While you're on hold, for example, use the time to address envelopes, prepare an agenda, or read junk mail. As you drive, think about the letter you have to write the minute you get to the office. By the time you get there, the letter will be done.

- **Do your most unpleasant task first.** As Mark Twain said, "If you have to swallow a frog, don't stare at it too long!"

- **Keep a "to do" list if you aren't already doing so.** Research shows you can increase your productivity by one-third if you have clearly determined prioritized work.

Manage Meetings

Time is money. If you're not getting your money's worth from the meetings you attend, do something about it. Here are four recommendations to help you define the aim of meetings, confine the resources that must be expended to meet the aim, and refine your meeting skills.

- **First, decide whether the meeting is truly necessary.** There are numerous other ways to exchange or create information, particularly in this age of technology.

- **Be sure there is an agenda that will govern the time allocated to the topic under discussion.** Confine discussion to the agenda items. The items should have the number of minutes to be spent on each one written in parentheses beside them. (Note: If you are planning the agenda, you can use your time estimation skills. Think through how you will break up that hour according to what needs to be accomplished. Align your desires with available resources—time in this case.)

Queryoid

What would your boss say about your skills?

- **Appoint a time and topic monitor.** This person has the authority to keep others on track within time allocations.

- **Assess the meeting periodically.** If little is being accomplished, stop holding meetings and find another way to obtain and disseminate the needed information.

Demand a Product From Training

Quite possibly your training department will object to producing a product. It may mean more work for the trainers if they volunteer to type the product before it is distributed. On the other hand, they may applaud the idea. Nonetheless, you should always leave a training session with the following three things:

- Greater knowledge and/or improved skills

- Materials prepared by the instructor in advance of the class

- Some "product" created during the class by participants, to be used once training is completed

The product will serve as visible proof that the learning can be immediatly applied. On the following pages are actual examples of products created by participants in a management class for the Bureau of Indian Affairs, Division of Accounting Management, Central Office West in Albuquerque, New Mexico.

To Leadership Class Attendees

Thank you for the seriousness with which you responded to our recent training and the wealth of good ideas you generated. Those collective efforts are contained in the following pages.

To Extend Training From the Classroom to the Workplace

1. Share materials with staff.

2. Conduct follow-up training sessions.

3. Set standards for meetings.

4. Develop liberal standards for using a team approach.

5. Publish the results of work teams.

6. Set up a special bulletin board.

7. Advertise requests for team members for special projects.

8. Have an application form for interested applicants.

9. Ensure team members' work is considered at evaluation time.

10. Determine criteria for team projects.

11. Insist agendas are used for all team meetings.

12. Arrange for supervisors who attended training to teach subordinates what they learned.

13. Ensure instructions are well-defined and clarified as needed.

14. Raise expectations for all employees.

15. Allow employees, and expect employees, to practice new skills.

16. Be generous with praise.

17. Start every meeting with an ice breaker.

18. Use teams more often.

19. Work to resolve conflicts within two days.

20. Keep employees informed.

21. Demonstrate patience as teams grow.

22. Respect all employees.

23. Have ground rules for all meetings.

24. Keep all meetings under one hour.

25. Look for alternatives to meetings.

26. Allocate a five-minute period at each staff meeting for transferring knowledge acquired in training.

Transference of Learning Plan

"I can and will support implementation of this team plan."

Signed by Ken Russell, John Weston, Linda Morris, Annie Walton, Mona Infield, Robert Thompson, and Dale Bajema

1. Train Staff in Team Building

   - Identify trainers.

   - Have a lesson plan.

   - Obtain permission to reproduce materials. (Chief)

   - Schedule training for staff. (Supervisors)

   - Conduct training. (Trainers)

2. Set Team Standards

   - Develop standards from training sessions. (Best of the Best)

   - Formalize standards. (Chief)

   - Display standards in training rooms.

3. Determine What Constitutes Initial Team Projects

   - Best of the Best proposals go to management after trainees have selected them.

   - Future projects come from management or are approved by management.

   - Management prioritizes projects.

   - Projects are advertised on a special bulletin board.

   - Staff proposes to work on teams.

   - Management selects team leader.

- Team leader selects team.

- Selection has management concurrence.

4. Team Results

  - Team's findings are placed on bulletin board.

  - Leaders send team member contributions to supervisors.

  - Summaries of team results are published in a newsletter.

  - Database is set up to record results.

  - Results are rewarded.

  - Method for evaluating team efforts is established in spirit of continuous improvement of operations.

Developing an Agenda

Considerations from Herman Redhouse, Ed Socks, Tom Mark, Hazel Paul, Donny Cannon, Cece Curley, Kaye Concho, and Steve Abeita

I. Format

   A. Date

   B. Time

   C. Place

   D. Purpose

      1. Participants

      2. Topics

II. Ground Rules

   A. Conduct

   B. Time awareness

   C. Positions (recorder, facilitator, time keeper)

III. Conclusion

   A. Decisions

   B. Unresolved issues

   C. Action plans

Considerations for Ground Rules

1. No meeting without an agenda

2. No personal attacks

3. Predetermined time and place

4. Mission statement

5. Time limits

6. No interruptions

7. Principal attendees or suitable alternates

8. Promptness

9. Facilitator and recorder selected at start of meeting

10. Rules defined

11. Process to resolve conflict

12. Agreement on how voting will be conducted

13. Agreement on extent of leader's involvement

Forms for Evaluating Meetings

From Delores Chaney, Bill Benjamin, Jim Barton, Henry Monarco, and Fran Drapeau

Yes   No

☐   ☐   1.   Was the purpose of the meeting clear?

☐   ☐   2.   Do you know why you were invited to the meeting?

☐   ☐   3.   Were the objectives of the meeting accomplished?

☐   ☐   4.   Was your time well spent?

☐   ☐   5.   Would you have attended this meeting if it were not required?

Other comments: _____

_____

_____

_____

_____

_____

_____

_____

_____

_____

From Frank Fricke, Grace Monarco, Marie Gorman, Gordon Babby, Henry Cooper, and Gerald Lucero

Yes No

☐ ☐ 1. Could this meeting have been held at a better time?

☐ ☐ 2. Were we on track?

☐ ☐ 3. Should we continue meeting?

☐ ☐ 4. Should others be involved in our meetings?

☐ ☐ 5. Was the meeting an appropriate length?

☐ ☐ 6. Did we cover too much?

☐ ☐ 7. Was the leader effective?

Suggestions for improvement: _____

_____

_____

_____

_____

_____

_____

_____

_____

_____

_____

Proposal

Changing Schedule From Five 8-hour Days to Four 10-hour Days

From Dale Bajema, Cece Curley, John Weston, Mona Infield, and Steve Abeita

Benefits:

1. More productive. Employees can concentrate on tasks for a longer period of time.

2. More personal time off. Employees will automatically have perpetual three-day weekends.

3. Less absenteeism. People will think twice about calling in sick as they will lose ten hours instead of eight.

4. Possible elimination of overtime.

5. Increased morale.

6. More leave can be saved for contingencies.

Likely objections and responses to them:

1. Problem covering the office on business days.

   Response: Cross-training of employees to cover each other. Employees must commit in writing to new schedule.

2. Problem with scheduling meetings or training.

   Response: Internal meetings will be held only on Tuesday, Wednesday, or Thursday.

Modify agreement for employee to work the five-day week during training periods.

Supply interchangeable resource for meetings that cannot be held these days.

3. What about being out of town for meetings? Will the ten-hour day apply?

Response: Take other work with you.

4. How do we decide who gets Monday or Friday off?

Response: Rotate in the case of conflict.

Schedule for implementation:

Proposal and comment period: 5 working days

Trial period: 6 weeks for all employees

Implementation period: Immediately following the trial period, barring catastrophes

Reevaluation time: 6 months and 1 year

Needed: Positive advertising in order to influence others

Proposal

Training Program

From Frank Fricke, Henry Monarco, Henry Cooper, Jim Barton, and Gil Chebahtah

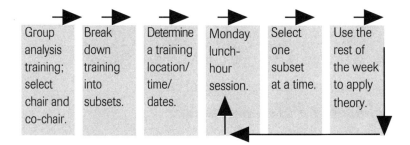

| Group analysis training; select chair and co-chair. | Break down training into subsets. | Determine a training location/ time/ dates. | Monday lunch-hour session. | Select one subset at a time. | Use the rest of the week to apply theory. |

Action Plan:

1. Discuss one subject.

2. Break subject into subsets.

3. Apply theory throughout the week.

4. On Monday of the next week, review the previous subject and select the next one.

5. Establish a collective telephone listing of people to contact for information.

Proposal

Electronic Bulletin Board With Official Information on Budget Cuts and Proposed RIF's

From Ed Socks, Donny Cannon, Tom Mark, Kaye Concho, and Hazel Paul

Benefits:

1. All employees would have current information.

2. Stress levels would be lowered.

Likely objections and responses to them:

1. The bulletin board would not be available to all.

   Response: Locate personal computers for those who need access; set up in common area.

Schedule for implementation:

1. As soon as possible. Equipment is available now.

2. Appoint a key person in each department.

Factoid

Forty-three percent of surveyed employees believe they are writing unnecessary reports.

▼

"Playing on the Office Team"

An article by Ken Russell, Annie Walton, and Ed Socks with a modicum of editorial assistance

Rules of the Game

Jack Stack has written about the "great game of business." In the more microcosmic sense, there is a great game to be played in the office as well. It's called "teamwork." And, like all games, it is governed by specific rules. We call those rules ground rules, a set of standards to which we expect team members' behavior to conform. In essence, the rules center around this maxim: "Treat time and each other with respect."

Specific applications of the essential maxim might be the following:

- Avoid personal attacks.

- Listen to one another.

- Deal with facts, not emotion.

- Use "straight talk."

Will there be barriers? Of course. Life without challenges is a bland succession of temporal segments. The effective team overcomes the barriers. The ineffective team succumbs to them. Like winning sports teams, effective office teams recognize the wide range of sources that might constitute barriers. For the sports team, the barriers could be psychological, physical, or atmospheric. For the office team, the barriers could be erected by co-workers, by management, by subordinates, by a lack of resources, and so on. The trick is not to wish for barrierless conditions. The trick is to welcome the opportunity to overcome adversity and to recognize and reward the attempts to do so. Attitude, as they say, is all.

Positions

There are four positions, aligned with the "4 P's of Effective Teamwork":

- *Power,* held by the team leader

- *Progress,* for which the facilitator is primarily responsible

- *Public Memory,* which is what the recorder or scribe captures

- *Participation,* which is expected of every team member

Additionally, each member of the team must, on occasion, play other positions for brief periods. For example, if the team seems to be heading toward "group think" (collective agreement too quickly reached), someone on the team should play the role of devil's advocate. If friction seems to be brewing between two members, any other member can step in and play the role of minister in order to soothe ruffled feathers. If too much verbiage is being issued on a simple point, the surgeon can step in and cut away the verbal fat.

Goals

The goal of all games is to win. In an office setting, "winning" means accomplishing the task with a minimum of waste and a maximum of positive effects. The task may be one suggested by upper management or one that the team itself has determined as a necessary course of action. Just as a team needs a coach, so too should the team have a coach to champion its cause.

Factoid

One-third of our files could be eliminated with no negative impact on our efficiency.

Quotoid

Marie Curie:
"One never
notices what
has been done;
one can only
see what
remains to be
done."

The team needs cheerleaders as well. There should be private encouragements when the team is dispirited and public displays when the team is successful.

Team Spirit

It is not a perfect world. Tensions do erupt, and emotions do get out of hand. Conflict is to be expected. It can, however, be controlled and channeled in a positive direction. The more practice team members have in dealing with conflict, the more easily the conflict can be directed to positive, "spirited" ends. Having team spirit also means having commitment. Each team member must ask if he or she is willing to make the commitment required. If not, perhaps this is neither the team nor the time to be involved.

Accept Paradoxes

We live in the Age of Paradox, when we are asked to do more with less. We are shrinking our world yet expanding our transglobal connections, gaining access to more and more information yet acquiring less and less knowledge. We have more labor-saving devices than ever before but less time to operate them. We are given empowerment and yet feel powerless in the face of corporate decisions. We communicate more it seems, but understand less; retire earlier but are unable to fill our spare time.

These paradoxes won't disappear. These contradictions, in fact, will probably grow, forcing us to develop skills of flexibility and adaptability. (Look at how easily we have adapted to computers and cellular phones, faxes and modems.) Similarly, we can teach ourselves to thrive in an environment hallmarked by chaos.

It's merely a question of shifting long-held paradigms in which security dominated our thinking. When you stop changing, it is said, you stop.

Although the Bureau of Indian Affairs is in a state of flux, as is every government agency, you saw hope in the proposals—hope and a desire to continuously improve despite changes in the basic structure and mission of their organization.

Determine your willingness to handle change and the upheavals it brings by completing the following quiz.

Quiz:
How Do You Feel About Change?

Place an X on the continuum to indicate your current disposition toward adaptive behavior.

1. I find change exciting and filled with the possibility of opportunity.

Not at all   Sometimes   Absolutely true of me

2. I do not feel threatened by the prospect of having to find a new job.

Not at all   Sometimes   Absolutely true of me

3. I enjoy learning new things and meeting new people.

Not at all   Sometimes   Absolutely true of me

4. I can tolerate chaos.

Not at all   Sometimes   Absolutely true of me

5. I am self-confident regarding my abilities.

Not at all   Sometimes   Absolutely true of me

6. I believe there are more questions than answers.

Not at all   Sometimes   Absolutely true of me

7. I regard myself as a risk-taker.

Not at all   Sometimes   Absolutely true of me

8. I like to experiment.

Not at all   Sometimes   Absolutely true of me

9. I enjoy challenges.

Not at all   Sometimes   Absolutely true of me

10. I look for the positive in every situation, every person.

Not at all   Sometimes   Absolutely true of me

Factoid

By the year 2000, according to the Department of Labor, 44 percent of all American employees will be working in data services.

Analyzing the Results:

A quick glance at the pattern of your X's will give you an indication of your willingness to "go with the flow." If the majority of your responses fall on the left side, it simply means you are still tethered to the status quo. Confine the amount of energy you expend trying to preserve the status quo. Try to wean yourself away from it, because the status simply will not remain "quo" for very much longer.

Summary

The individual action plan that is outlined and explained in Chapter 4 is extended in this chapter—extended to time, meetings, and training.

Time is the most precious commodity. To spend it in addictive ways is certainly acceptable—provided you have no other important priorities you should be spending it on.

Management of time is the key. Estimating the time that will be allotted to a given task is one way to assume mastery of days that seem out of control. You may have heard of Parkinson's Law: Work expands to the amount of time we give it. There is an opposite law as well, called the Confinement Law: Work contracts to the amount of time you allocate for its completion.

Managing the meetings you attend and convene is another way to confine the resources being expended to accomplish tasks. Ask first if the meeting is necessary. If so, insist there be an agenda (with time allocations written in parentheses beside each item on the agenda). Ensure that time and topic monitors are appointed. These individuals keep the meeting on track, using the indicated time frames posted beside the agenda items. Ground rules also help keep the meeting focused on the intentions targeted on the agenda. These rules confine team members to speaking only about the topic under discussion or speaking only for a prescribed amount of time.

Quotoid

Today there are nearly 27 million more e-mail addresses than there were in 1987.

Factoid

American firms spend $30 billion on training annually.

▼

Periodically assess your meetings. The feedback enables the leader to make further refinements and confinements for future meetings.

The amount of energy and effort expended on the organization's behalf must be confined to the most productive outcomes. One way to make this happen is to create products within training sessions. These products can and will be used later, and they serve as a record of what was learned and proposed. Several excellent examples of ways to transfer training from the classroom to the workplace were provided by trainees from the Bureau of Indian Affairs.

Finally, you were encouraged to confine the amount of time, energy, and worry that you spend seeking to maintain the existing order. Change is inevitable, and the pace of that change seems to increase daily. The more adaptive you are, the more you can direct your energies—not to hold on to the past but rather to prepare for the future.

Interview with Christina Schmittner, Executive Administrator, Wall Street firm, New York, New York

Factoid

An average of 145 pages come across your desk each week.

In the past, especially in a large bureaucratic organization, information was extremely formalized and paperwork was outrageous. The arrival of electronic mail had a significant impact on paperwork. It allows us to receive important information in an informal manner.

To keep from being entrapped by details, I organize my daily work flow and categorize the information I receive.

Further, I disseminate information and follow up on items as soon as possible. Do not allow things to build up— they must be done sooner or later anyway. Do them sooner.

I try to follow this simple rule: "Gain a piece of paper, lose a piece of paper." There should always be something to throw away.

Decline

6

Having refined a plan and made overtures to confine the waste often associated with meetings, training, and time, you are now in a position to develop the skill of declining people and invitations that intrude upon your best intentions if you let them. One of the best ways to stick to your goal-guns is to decide what must be done in a given hour or a given day. When other forces try to steal your attention, learn to turn them away, without turning a cold shoulder.

For example, you are tempted to take an art class but know that your days are already full with work during the day and earning a degree at night and on weekends. But, you have a strong desire and find yourself reading

2

Factoid

Ten thousand
new jobs a day
are created in
the United
States—
mostly in the
"knowledge
work" sector.

▼

catalogs and filling out enrollment forms. Don't deny the desire. Instead, subjugate it to a more appropriate time and place.

Buy a five-year calendar, decide when current responsibilities will lessen, and then record when you will find time to follow a mini-dream. In the meantime, put all the material related to a particular interest in a separate file, to be examined as the relevant date approaches. That's what Rick Best does (see interview at the end of this chapter). You can temporarily decline the urge to study art without denying the need to pursue it.

Learn to Say "No"

One of the best ways to keep your head above the ever-cresting waves of data is to learn to say "no" to the following:

- To those who would waste your time as they waste their own.

- To all those new books on the market until you have read all those you already have.

- To invitations to events you really do not wish to attend.

- To reports you don't need to read.

- To meetings from which you can learn little.

- To those who want you on their mailing lists.

- To Internet connections unless they have value to you.

Telephone Terminators

Another way that useless information may be cluttering your life is the telephone conversation. People who belabor their points and who keep you tied up with meaningless chatter need to be declined—graciously but firmly. The best advice is probably to have a list such as the following near your phone. These cut-off points are called "The Terminators."

Factoid

The average American receives the equivalent of 41 pounds of junk mail a year.

- "I'd like to hear more, but I have to get this report finished."

- "I know you well enough to tell you that I don't have time to talk any longer."

- "Excuse me for interrupting, but if I don't finish this budget, my boss will hit the ceiling."

- "Save it for the next time I see you. I've got to work on this layout."

- "Oh, my secretary just walked in with a stack of messages. I'd better get going."

- "I don't want to take up any more of your time. It's been good talking to you."

- "I'll let you go now so you can get back to work."

The dictionary definition of *decline* is to refuse to accept or do something, especially in a way that is formally polite. "Be ruthless with time but gracious with people" is a maxim by which efficient time managers live. Use the following exercise to practice gracefully saying "no."

Exercise:
Saying "No" Gracefully

As always, there's a right way and a wrong way to conduct your interpersonal interactions. Look at the wrong ways below and rewrite the statements so the decliner is doing what he or she feels is important without diminishing the importance of the person being declined.

1. When someone is dominating a meeting

   Wrong way: Joan, why don't you shut up? You've been yammering for the last ten minutes. You haven't said anything we don't already know.

   Right way: _____

   _____

2. When someone is "chewing you out"

   Wrong way: I don't get paid enough to listen to junk like this.

   Right way: _____

   _____

3. When someone is socializing excessively:

   Wrong way: Tim, do you really think I care what color tu-tu your daughter wore at her ballet recital?

   Right way: _____

   _____

Refuse to Read Every Word (Unless It's a Legal Document)

As the rate of information input increases, you must learn to read more efficiently to keep up. The proliferation of messages alone has made speed reading necessary as a means of surviving. As Cliff High of Tenax Software Engineering reports, "Ninety percent of all e-mail I get gets dumped into the trash can. The faster I can read into the first few lines, the faster I can dispose of it." Mr. High has actually developed software that displays e-mail files in chunks of 16 characters at a time—the optimum speed for the human eye. Thus, he has reduced his e-mail reading from three hours to half an hour each day. (Reprinted with permission from the August 1995 issue of *Training Magazine*. Copyright 1995. Lakewood Publications, Minneapolis, MN. All rights reserved. Not for resale.)

The suggestions below will assist you in increasing your speed-reading ability:

- **Ask questions about the material before you begin to read it.** Knowing what you are looking for helps you focus on the intended message.

- **Make a game of it.** Predict what the material is going to say and then confirm your prediction, or let the material surprise you.

- **Don't vocalize.** In other words, don't move your lips as you read—it slows you down.

- **Allow yourself to skip over words.** Try to glean the main idea. For example, most free-lance writers know that when they spot the words "regret" or "unfortunately" in the first sentence of a would-be publisher's letter, they really don't have to read the rest of the letter.

- **Measure yourself.** Use a time clock as you read one full newspaper column. Each day, read a column of comparable length and record your time to learn if you are picking up speed.

Refuse to Write Every Word (Unless It's a Legal Document)

Those with perfectionist tendencies or teaching backgrounds tend to elaborate and even overelaborate the points they wish to make. There are others, too, who simply have not learned the K-I-S-S principle: "Keep It Simple, Silly." To illustrate, if you begin a memo with these words—"The purpose of this memo is to advise you that ..."—you have wasted ten words and precious reading time. To illustrate further, imagine the noneffectiveness of "No Parking" or school crossing signs with those ten bloated words preceding them.

If you can master the following four recommendations, you will be able to reduce your verbiage by approximately 50 percent without sacrificing meaning. Thus, you will save writing time, the cost of transmission (whether paper, fax, e-mail is being used), and the reader's time.

- **Don't waste words at the beginning.** Get right to the point.

- **Eliminate as many wimpy verbs and passive-voice verbs as you can.** Replace them with strong action verbs. A wimpy verb is a word like "is."

- **A passive-voice verb has a wimpy verb in front of a past-tense verb form**. "Has been found" and "will be written" are examples of passive-voice verbs.

- **Look for action hiding in a noun.** If you change this sentence: "A decision will be made by the financial officer" to this sentence: "The financial officer will decide" you have found the action (*decide*) hiding in the noun (*decision*) and you have reduced your verbiage by nearly 50 percent.

- **Eliminate as many prepositional phrases as you can.** They make your writing sound choppy and childlike. Worse yet, they make your sentences unnecessarily long. Can you convert the following long-winded sentence (thirty-three words) to a mere nine words without altering the meaning at all? By following the previous recommendations, you can convert verbosity to verve—and reduce the number of words by nearly 75 percent.

There is a great deal of cooperation on the part of the employees of the ABC Company of New York with the employees of the DEF Company of Albuquerque at the present time.

Need some help? Here's one possible answer: *New York's ABC Company cooperates with Albuquerque's DEF Company.*

Factoid

A daily copy of the New York Times *has more information than someone living in England in the 1600s would have seen in a lifetime.*

▼

Refuse to Save Every Word (Unless It's a Legal Document)

There are knowledge misers, to be sure, those who approach information like pack rats. They truly enjoy collecting, hoarding, and using data. You can spot them easily—their eyes are often blurred from excess reading, their bookshelves are bulging, their files outnumber everyone else's, and their computer file lists are longer than anyone else's.

If you fall into (or even if you are on the outskirts of) this distinction, one simple trick is to discard the elements preceeding the final product. Just as painters throw away the preliminary sketches once the final drawing is complete, so too should knowledge workers eliminate the building blocks that helped the final document be built.

Refuse to Attend Every Conference

Your boss will no doubt appreciate your cost-saving efforts as you suggest purchasing the printed conference proceedings instead of being physically present at a conference. If you make this suggestion, prepare a breakdown of the savings. (Of course, this idea works only if you're truly interested in obtaining meaningful information as opposed to taking a week off work to visit an alluring city.)

Learn to Be Selective

Wilfredo Pareto was an Italian economist of the 1800s who discovered what has since been called The Pareto Principle. In essence, it says that a minority of the total causes constitutes the majority of the effect. The ratio is roughly 20/80. So if you do ten tasks today at work, two of them will create the major impact (80 percent worth) on the customer or the mission you seek to accomplish.

The ratio is a useful guide to help determine which of your actions will be the most significant. To illustrate, if you have ten articles you want to read, decide which two titles have the greatest relevance to the work you do. Read those carefully and skim the remaining eight.

By applying this mental yardstick in advance of whatever you do, you can assess and select from the actions that always outnumber the amount of time available.

Given the new skills and ideas you are acquiring with each chapter of this book, you may wish to revisit your action plan from time to time and include some specific techniques you would like to make part of your standard operating procedure.

Learn to Relinquish Perfectionism

We've been raised to be diligent in all that we undertake. And—here is the paradox—given the overwhelming amount of work that lies in wait for most of us, we are forced to do some things less thoroughly than we would like. This is not to say you should be careless or lack attention to detail. But—if you must get out three documents today and you have time to do only two with

Factoid

Each year, 11,000 magazines are published in the United States.

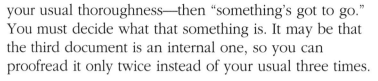

Factoid

Seventy-eight percent of Americans feel time moves too fast for them.

▼

your usual thoroughness—then "something's got to go." You must decide what that something is. It may be that the third document is an internal one, so you can proofread it only twice instead of your usual three times.

Reengineering the processes by which work is handled may be called for if you are to juggle the demands of customers for high quality with the demands of time.

Summary

Life offers many choices. We cannot take them all. Keep this advice in mind at all times—whether you're in a restaurant looking at an unending menu, or in a clothing store faced with competing attractions. No one can have it all, do it all, see it all, or read it all. Life, quite simply, is a question of making choices.

We accept some invitations, we decline others. As we do so, the familiar time-management maxim should guide us: "Be ruthless with time but gracious with people."

Projecting our hopes, intentions, and goals ahead to a five-year period will gently remind us of priorities—particularly if we record them on a five-year calendar. Folders help, too, as does the ability to say "no."

Furthermore, you can refuse to read every word, write every word, save every word. And you can loosen the stranglehold perfectionism has on you.

Quotoid

Clarence Randall: "Facts are working tools only."

Interview with Rick Best, founder, Delphi Training and Development, Ontario, California

I don't actually swim in the sea of information. I dog paddle, perhaps, but mostly tread water. Swimming connotes to me swift, graceful, almost effortless movement, the purpose of which is relaxation. Dog paddling or treading water, on the other hand, suggests keeping my head above water to survive.

Whether at work or at home, I find myself inundated with information. The issue for me has become one of collecting and organizing information that addresses my immediate concerns and screening out the information that does not.

At work, my secretary opens my mail and separates it into two folders—that which needs my immediate attention and that which I can review at leisure. I read that which requires my attention early in the day while I am fresh and can rearrange my priorities. I use a tickler file for action items due later.

The other mail I read during low energy periods in the week. Journals, junk mail, and advertisements are quickly scanned to see if they are directed at current projects, or those I expect to be involved in. If not, they are thrown away or routed to others who may be interested. I cut out articles that apply to current projects to read during other low-energy periods and discard the rest of the journal. Keeping only pertinent articles reduces the physical size of my reading file.

For projects due later, I collect articles, books, studies, and proposals and file them. I schedule a block of time for reading them near the project's due date. I find that I read much more efficiently with a due date near.

I use similar techniques at home. Junk mail is thrown away unopened unless it is clear from the envelope that it is relevant to my personal interests. I scan the newspaper's index to identify articles of interest and only read the first few paragraphs unless the details are especially important. Most of my other reading is project-oriented and is accomplished in specified blocks of time.

Factoid

More than 1.5 trillion pieces of paper are circulated each year in American offices.

7

Outline

Electronic media make everyone a communicator. The mind sometimes begs for mercy as it faces the wide array of data being swept our way each minute. Our very sanity sometimes hangs in balance between the learning required and the time left to use what we have acquired.

Without doing some sort of internal screening, that is, assessing how the tasks and information confronting you fit into the context of the bigger picture, you will feel like the mythical Sisyphus, who struggled to roll a huge boulder to the top of a mountain—only to have it roll right back down again. Do you sometimes feel that no matter how hard you work, no matter how much paperwork you clear away by the end of the day, when you return to work in the morning, the piles start to grow again (and wind up bigger than they were before). This image of never reaching the top of the paperwork mountain is a realistic image, as the following exercise illustrates.

Draw two circles below. The first should represent the amount of knowledge you have about the work you do. The second should represent how much knowledge currently exists related to the work you do.

Now draw a circle five times bigger than the second one on the previous page.

The largest circle, experts tell us, represents the amount of information concerning your job that will exist in the next five years. (Compare your original circle, reflecting your degree of knowledge about your field to the five-times-bigger circle.)

We can't keep information from exploding. We can only devise means to survive among the chunks of data being hurtled through space as a result of the explosion.

It becomes necessary to rapidly assess information and then outline it to optimize its value. (Note how the proposals from the Bureau of Indian Affairs were outlined in chapter 5.) Here are some suggestions to get you started.

Use Visual Maps

One of the best ways to store information—mentally or physically—is with a visual map. Visual maps can help you outline and organize the critical aspects of the information that floods you. They force you to decide in an instant how information will be used. They require you to determine whether the information is important enough for a category of its own or whether you should place it in another category.

There are numerous types of visual maps. Several are explored here.

1. **Sectioning.** This technique involves taking a topic that seems unwieldy to you and breaking it into eight to ten sections that capture the essence of the topic. Each of these sections would be represented by a large rectangle (see accompanying diagram).

   To illustrate, assume your boss has asked you to deliver a half-hour presentation at the next staff meeting, which will include several new hires in the department. Your topic is "How this department works and what it produces." You would write each main topic in capital letters above each of the sections.

How This Department Works and What It Produces

TRAINING

Arrange scheduling	

An example of sectioning.

As you write your section headings, no doubt other less-encompassing ideas will come to mind. You would write these in lowercase letters in the appropriate section. For example, if you are part of the Human Resources Department, TRAINING will probably be one of the sections. But the thought "arrange scheduling" may pop up. You would subsume it in its proper place—as one of the lowercase entries in the main section.

Sectioning typically takes minutes to do and leaves you with orderly definitions and depictions of the larger picture. You can then begin files for each of the major sections and, as papers cross your desk, you can easily and neatly relegate them to their proper place. Or, as in the hypothetical example, you will have in a matter of minutes more than enough information to present in a half-hour presentation.

2. **NUN Technique.** Before deciding to keep, acquire, or listen to incoming information, quickly assess it using this technique. It involves asking three questions before bringing more data into your life.

- Is this **N**eed-to-know information?

- Is this **U**nnecessary information?

- Is this **N**ice-to-know information?

Think NUN before typing or digesting e-mail, letters, reports, and other information-laden material.

3. Parallel priorities. At least once a year, sit down with your boss to determine whether your priorities are truly shared priorities. Begin by answering these questions yourself.

- What am I paid to do?

- Of all the activities I engage in during a typical week, which has the top priority?

- If someone were to replace me tomorrow, what qualifications would he or she need to do my job as well as I do it?

- What is the worst mistake I could make on this job?

- What obstacles prevent me from doing the best work I am capable of doing?

- What is my boss's top priority?

- Which of my tasks provides the most value to internal customers? to external customers?

- How would our CEO say I should be spending most of my time?

Next, without showing your supervisor the answers you wrote, ask him or her to answer the same questions regarding you and the way you perform your job.

Finally, arrange a meeting for you and your boss to compare your answers and agree on parallel priorities. Subsequently, as information passes through your working days, mentally flash back to the answers the two of you decided on and act accordingly.

Factoid

Executives waste up to three and a half months each year on distractions (mostly meetings that are not necessary).

Queryoid

Do you use visual maps?

▼

4. **N²Y².** One popular technique for making decisions that have an ethical base is to ask the following:

- "Will this action harm anyone else?"
- "Will it harm me?"
- "Will it benefit anyone else?"
- "Will it benefit me?"

You should be able to answer "no" to the first two questions and "yes" to the last two.

A variation on this is the N²Y² *model*. As information comes across your desk in the future, imagine the following grid and the four questions. If you can give two "no" answers and then two "yes" answers, you probably have a legitimate foundation for incorporating this information into your knowledge base.

	No	Yes
Does our organization have this information?	✔	
Do I have this information?	✔	
Can this benefit the organization?		✔
Can it benefit me?		✔

When you have to decide on the worth of more information you are tempted to amass, picture this diagram. If you can answer two "no's" and two "yeses" as shown in the model, you will know whether or not to add more data to your existing collection.

Success, as nineteenth-century painter James Whistler defined it, means "knowing what not to put in." And your success, in very large measure, will depend on what goes "in" to your work "out"line.

Advance the Action

Just as you must outline and organize the information you encounter each day—first, to see if it fits into the big picture and if you really need it, and then to organize it if you do need it—you must also outline your time to ensure that each of your priorities moves forward.

Ideally, you have already mapped out what is due when and have a chart or file for each project, with milestone dates clearly indicated. The following time guidelines will help you advance the action to leave each project at the end of the day a little further along the path to completion than it was at the beginning of your workday. You will expend some energy each day to move each project along.

- Spend approximately three hours a day on work due today.

- Spend approximately three hours a day on work due next week.

- Spend approximately one hour a day on work due next month.

Factoid

Each day, 750 million computer-generated pages are printed.

- Spend approximately a half hour a day on work due in six months.

- Spend leftover minutes each day on work due next year.

Next, make a list of all the work you have to do. (For the moment, pay no attention to due dates.)

Then, for each item you listed, indicate when the work is due. This projection will make you aware of what must be done and how to allocate time during your workdays. Keep your list in front of you to resist the pull of info-magnets.

Envision the Idealized State

Envisioning the ideal and then determining a plan for making it real is another method of outlining.

Psychologist Kurt Lewin has provided improvement seekers such as yourself a useful tool for reaching an improved state of affairs. It requires you to consider the difference between "what is" and "what could be." It works, however, only if you believe it is possible to be a more efficient information processor than you currently are.

The tool, called Force Field Analysis, works like this with regard to Info-Flood. First, describe the flood of information that currently inundates your life (both work and personal). Be specific. List the kinds of information, where it comes from, and how often. Next, describe what you're doing to deal with it. Then envision how you would ideally handle the information (e.g., what resources would you need?). Finally, create an outline containing the steps you can take to close the gap between the real and the ideal.

Try the Force Field Analysis technique for yourself in the following exercise.

Quotoid

Marilyn Peterson: "If it isn't at the 7-Eleven, I don't need it."

▼

1. Describe the Info-Flood that currently inundates your work and personal life. (What kinds of information, from what sources, how often received, etc.?)

_____

_____

_____

_____

_____

_____

_____

_____

2. Describe what you do to stay afloat.

_____

_____

_____

_____

_____

_____

_____

_____

_____

3. Envision the ideal state and describe it here. In other words, if you handled the flood like a seasoned "sailor," what would you be doing, with what resources?

_____

_____

_____

_____

_____

_____

_____

4. What can you do to close the gap between the real and the ideal? Prepare an outline showing what you can and will do.

_____

_____

_____

_____

_____

_____

_____

Predictoid

By 2040, the Yale Library will have 200 million titles on 6,000 miles of shelves.

◀

Quotoid

*Warren Bennis:
"The factory of
the future will
have only two
employees—a
man and a dog.
The man will be
there to feed
the dog. The
dog will be
there to keep
the man from
touching the
equipment."*

Summary

We live in a networked world—as individuals, and as corporate citizens. The amount of information we have access to is truly staggering. As you have obviously realized, the sprawl needs to be contained. Learn to assess and assimilate information in terms of an outline— that is, with the big picture or overall topic in mind. Information you encounter is placed into the major "outline" categories. Discard information that isn't a match.

When you keep the big picture in mind at all times, you're constantly aware of the purpose behind your actions. Having that inner voice whispering in your ear enables you to quickly decide how to deal with the numerous documents and chunks of information that tug at you.

Visual maps are good tools for "outlining" the data that bombard us each day. In this chapter, four were recommended: *Sectioning* allows you to allocate bits of information to appropriate categories. *NUN* provides you with a method for questioning the necessity of expanding your knowledge base. *Parallel Priorities* ensures that you and your supervisors are focusing on the same key elements. Finally, N^2Y^2 helps you quickly assess information before you let it enter your knowledge base.

You can outline your time to ensure that each of your priorities moves forward each day. This gives you a sense of accomplishment and helps you avoid last-minute deadline crunches.

Envisioning the ideal and then determining how to make it real is another method of outlining.

Queryoid

Do you make self-pledges?

Factoid

You wear more computing power on your wrist than was available in the whole world before 1961.

▼

Interviews with employees of 10th Mountain Division, Fort Drum, NY

Leda Bond, Donna Heinzman, Paul Richer, Gary Douglas, and Kim Dehart

The following are techniques we have found useful for coping with Info-Angst:

- Prioritize types of information needed for tasks at hand or for future reference.

- Select sources of information wisely.

- Ignore what is superfluous and redundant.

- Discard unneeded and outdated information.

- Take what you need and leave the rest.

Mary Remsburg, Jee Fineout, Henry Avallone, Joe Margren, Tom Heiler

Information overload can be controlled by eliminating obsolete reference material or regulations. Focus upon and absorb current interests or job-related data. Listen to children if you wish to become apprised of new technologies or old. (They can tell you how to program your VCR.) Drop magazine subscriptions if you already know a great deal about the topics they present—subscribe to those that can tell you something new. If attending a meeting, review material just before the meeting. Trash any papers that are not relevant after you have skimmed them for content. The main point is to zero in on information you need. Use it or lose it.

Tammy Leeder, Violet Armour, Ronni Martinez, April Brigham, Cindy Gotham, Penny Guyette

To cope with information overload, you should first evaluate what information is necessary for you to have at the time versus what is "nice to know." Organize the available information so you are able to access it when you need it. Limit the time you spend absorbing information to avoid having it monopolize your time. Combine tasks—listen to the news while cleaning the car. Take "mental breaks," which will reduce stress and in turn help you acquire and apply the information you need.

Conclusion

In one way or another, each of the chapters in *Info-Flood* concentrates on shortcuts through the broadbands of information that can send you off in any number of directions. Each chapter encourages stripping away the trivia. Each emphasizes that if information is not managed and not managed well—individually and organizationally—then it is more of a liability than an asset.

Define (Chapter 1). Without knowledge, we cannot make intelligent choices. You were encouraged in this chapter to assess the areas where you need help coping with the sea of information. You were also encouraged to communicate—with yourself, with team members, and with organizational representatives so that concerted rescue efforts can be undertaken.

Align (Chapter 2). When wheels are out of alignment, the car pulls to the side. When your intentions aren't aligned with the direction in which colleagues, supervisors, and the firm itself are heading, you are wasting efforts (and possibly damaging your career). This chapter asked you to think strategically about your job,

Quotoid

Elizabeth
Barrett
Browning:
"Light
tomorrow with
today."

▼

your company, and your industry and then to parallel your own inclinations with emerging trends. Doing so will help you understand which information you should be paying attention to and acting upon.

Streamline (Chapter 3). In an ever-narrowing focus, *Info-Flood* proceeds to sharpen your thinking about what you do and how you do it. Priorities are emphasized here and numerous tips are presented for bringing clarity to your direction and intentions—all of this is a prelude to the important action plan that should be emerging.

Refine (Chapter 4). You ideally worked to create an action plan in this chapter, one that crystallized your previous thinking into a well-shaped projection for the future. A number of mental strands were probably being woven as a result of chapter tips and techniques. Here was your opportunity to refine those many ideas and sew them into a fabric that fits you.

Confine (Chapter 5). The inevitable paradoxes of contemporary living and working were confronted in this chapter, and suggestions for being adaptive, for creating coherence out of seeming chaos, were provided. Further tips for self-management, time management, and meeting management were provided, along with the recommendations to leave meetings and training sessions with tangible results.

Decline (Chapter 6). Saying "no" to self-imposed temptations and obligations others impose on us is stressed in this chapter. Ideally, a shift occurred in long-held views of how to read and write. The obsessive need to "have it all" was discouraged. It was supplanted by the need to take only what you need.

Outline (Chapter 7). Outlines help us distinguish information that is salient from that which is insignificant. Visual maps reflect the crux of this chapter. They help you decide which of the excessive details you encounter is relevant by stripping away irrelevancies. You can then make decisions accordingly.

Your Final Exam

Technological wonders can bedazzle us. The plethora of possibilities afforded by on-line services and the seemingly random organization of the knowledge base may blind us from finding the information we need in more traditional and often more convenient sources.

Notwithstanding this observation, however, it is a brave new world we are entering. And, like any new world, it beckons the brave who come with courage and cognizance of the dangerous attractions. Too much feeding at the information trough can be addictive. Too much of a good thing can be bad after all.

Clever cybernauts, though, are aware of the difference between information and knowledge. They know when to come in from the rain of data that can soak us. They seek techniques, such as those provided in these chapters, for easy sailing through the fact-filled waters of today's business world.

Let's see how well you've learned your lessons so far. If you read the review of the chapters and it sounded familiar and, better yet, if you found you have followed the chapter's guidelines, then you have increased your range of skills. Take the "Final Exam" that follows to see how much you've improved.

Factoid

Less than 3 percent of the American work force works in agriculture.

Final Exam

Answer the following questions using the most appropriate response:

A = Always

U = Usually

S = Sometimes

R = Rarely

N = Never

_____ 1. I believe I can control information rather than vice versa.

_____ 2. I can absorb information even if it's presented in short spurts.

_____ 3. I try to eliminate wasted effort.

_____ 4. At work, I go into "crisis mode" with deadlines.

_____ 5. I accomplish the goals I set each week.

_____ 6. My desk has "loose" items on it (messages, business cards).

_____ 7. I put projects off until the last minute.

_____ 8. I find ways to get rid of paper and paperwork.

_____ 9. My files have duplicate and outdated information.

_____ 10. Without question, I do what my boss asks me to do.

_____ 11. I force myself not to read, not to write every word.

_____ 12. I consciously assess information before assimilating it.

Interpreting your score:

For numbers 1, 2, 3, 5, 8, 11, and 12, give yourself these points:

A-4; U-3; S-2; R-1; N-0

For numbers 4, 6, 7, 9, and 10, give yourself these points:

A-0; U-1; S-2; R-3; N-4

Total: _____

Results:

36 or more: You've taken the suggestions to heart and possess the essential skills for navigating the turbulent waters without being flooded.

25-35: You're a good sailor but you may need refresher courses from time to time. Refer to this book periodically.

24 or less: You need to apply the tips and techniques on a more regular basis in order to avoid drowning.

No matter what your score, if you have read this book, you have learned. What you will do with your learning is entirely up to you. You are the captain of your own knowledge-boat. May the wind be always at your back and untroubled waters at your front.

Factoid

Managers use more than one ton of office paper annually.

Bibliography and Suggested Reading

Burrus, Daniel. *Technotrends: How to Use Technology to Go Beyond Your Competition*. New York: HarperBusiness, 1993.

Caroselli, Marlene. *Meetings That Work*. Mission, KS: SkillPath Publications, 1992.

Culp, Stephanie. *How to Get Organized When You Don't Have the Time*. Cincinnati, OH: Writer's Digest Book, 1986.

Depree, Max. *Leadership Is an Art*. New York: Doubleday, 1989.

Handy, Charles. *The Age of Paradox*. Boston, MS: Harvard Business School Press, 1994.

Hequet, Mark. "E-mail Spins a New Web at Work." *Training,* 32(8), 1995:56.

Johnson, Spencer. *Yes or No: The Guide to Better Decisions*. New York: HarperCollins, 1992.

Naisbitt, John, and Patricia Aburdene. *Megatrends 2000: Ten New Directions for the 1990's*. New York: Morrow, 1990.

Peters, Tom J. *The Tom Peters Seminar: Crazy Times Call for Crazy Organizations*. New York: Vintage Books, 1994.

Scholtes, Peter. *The Team Handbook: How to Use Teams to Improve Quality*. Madison, WI: Joiner Associates, 1988.

Stack, Jack. *The Great Game of Business*. New York: Doubleday, 1992.

Available From SkillPath Publications

Self-Study Sourcebooks

Climbing the Corporate Ladder: What You Need to Know and Do to Be a Promotable Person *by Barbara Pachter and Marjorie Brody*

Coping With Supervisory Nightmares: 12 Common Nightmares of Leadership and What You Can Do About Them *by Michael and Deborah Singer Dobson*

Defeating Procrastination: 52 Fail-Safe Tips for Keeping Time on Your Side *by Marlene Caroselli, Ed.D.*

Discovering Your Purpose *by Ivy Haley*

Going for the Gold: Winning the Gold Medal for Financial Independence *by Lesley D. Bissett, CFP*

Having Something to Say When You Have to Say Something: The Art of Organizing Your Presentation *by Randy Horn*

Info-Flood: How to Swim in a Sea of Information Without Going Under *by Marlene Caroselli, Ed.D.*

The Innovative Secretary *by Marlene Caroselli, Ed.D.*

Mastering the Art of Communication: Your Keys to Developing a More Effective Personal Style *by Michelle Fairfield Poley*

Organized for Success! 95 Tips for Taking Control of Your Time, Your Space, and Your Life *by Nanci McGraw*

A Passion to Lead! How to Develop Your Natural Leadership Ability *by Michael Plumstead*

P.E.R.S.U.A.D.E.: Communication Strategies That Move People to Action *by Marlene Caroselli, Ed.D.*

Productivity Power: 250 Great Ideas for Being More Productive *by Jim Temme*

Promoting Yourself: 50 Ways to Increase Your Prestige, Power, and Paycheck *by Marlene Caroselli, Ed.D.*

Proof Positive: How to Find Errors Before They Embarrass You *by Karen L. Anderson*

Risk-Taking: 50 Ways to Turn Risks Into Rewards *by Marlene Caroselli, Ed.D and David Harris*

Stress Control: How You Can Find Relief From Life's Daily Stress *by Steve Bell*

The Technical Writer's Guide *by Robert McGraw*

Total Quality Customer Service: How to Make It Your Way of Life *by Jim Temme*

Write It Right! A Guide for Clear and Correct Writing *by Richard Andersen and Helene Hinis*

Your Total Communication Image *by Janet Signe Olson, Ph.D.*

Handbooks

The ABC's of Empowered Teams: Building Blocks for Success *by Mark Towers*

Assert Yourself! Developing Power-Packed Communication Skills to Make Your Points Clearly, Confidently, and Persuasively *by Lisa Contini*

Breaking the Ice: How to Improve Your On-the-Spot Communication Skills *by Deborah Shouse*

For more information, call 1-800-873-7545.